101 Medieval Churches of West Sussex

A TOURING GUIDE

PAUL COPPIN

Illustrations by the Author, assisted by John Martin

S. B. Publications

ACKNOWLEDGEMENTS

My thanks go to: all the vicars, rectors and churchwardens who were only too pleased to show me round their churches especially those at Edburton, Itchingfield and Westhampnett. My very special thanks go to John Martin who assisted me both with the research and photography. Without John's hard work and innovative ideas this book would be a much poorer offering. Also to my wife for her help in correcting and compiling the finished article.

DEDICATION

This book is dedicated to my daughter Charlotte.
She has never given me cause for anything but pride.

First published in 2005 by S. B. Publications
Tel: 01323 893498
Email: sbpublications@tiscali.co.uk

ISBN 1-85770-306-5

Designed and Typeset by EH Graphics (01273) 515527
Printed by Ethos Productions Ltd.

CONTENTS

Front Cover: Yapton Church
Back Cover: Botolphs

INTRODUCTION

While working on my first book, on the churches of East Sussex, I was constantly amazed at the large number and rich variation of ancient churches in the county. Keen to continue my church research and photography I approached West Sussex expecting it to be much the same as its eastern brother. After all they were one large county in times past, how different could they be?

The answer is, very different. To start with West Sussex is the big brother, both in size and church numbers, more than half as many again as East Sussex. (I must at this point once again thank my good friend John Martin for the immense amount of help he gave me both in the research and in supplying several of the photos of the individual churches). Second the quality, East Sussex is good but West Sussex is superb, few if any counties in England can match it. From impressive Bosham and Boxgrove to tiny candlelit Greatham and Wiggonholt the variation is immense. This added another aspect to my book as I set out to find out why the two Sussex counties are so different when it comes to their church history. I soon discovered the significance of the giant forest that once cut the county off from the rest of England and the influence of the two major rivers flowing from the forest to the sea. The early Christian Saxon Kings to the west, the surviving Roman road system from Chichester and St Wilfrid have also played their part, perhaps St Wilfrid most of all.

One of the biggest surprises was the isolation of some of the churches, it has often been quite rewarding just to find the building and I envy the reader setting out to find some of the churches in this book for the first time.

I have once again interspersed the church sections with articles dealing with different aspects of churches and church life in an attempt to assist the visitor in getting the most out of a visit. My advice is don't rush, walk right round the church before going in, look at the ceiling and at the floor, poke your head in every corner or you will miss so much.

Many people have suggested the inclusion of a map and I thought long and hard, trying out several styles in the process. In the end I have settled for a small map at the start of each section as being the most helpful and least confusing, a county map identifying the areas is also included.

I have included the same rating system used in my first book; this rates each church by what they actually possess in three categories, settings, architectural features and linked history. There is also a 'top ten' based on this rating system.

Also included are recommended two and a half-hour tours for each area.

I am often asked about gaining access to churches. The answer is that most are open or the keys are readily available, some inevitably are kept locked as they contain valuable treasures. I would like to recommend the leaflet 'Sussex churches, Open in West Sussex' available from West Sussex County Council, although I must stress that this does not list all the open churches by any means. My advice is visit the church anyway, the external features alone are worth the visit. If you can gain access to a church so much the better and please sign the visitors book as this is often used to gauge whether or not to keep the church open. Also, bear in mind that the upkeep of the smallest church can cost over £100 per week, with some churches costing as much as £200 per day to run so please think of buying a guide book, post card or just dropping a few coins in the collection box.

Unlike East Sussex where there are almost exactly 101 medieval village churches, West Sussex has over 160 so it was necessary to pick 101 to include in this book. I have tried to choose a cross-section of churches offering a wide variation of examples. Once again I have avoided

the big towns and kept to the village churches for these reflect the slow evolution of the county better than the fast changing towns. There are no churches included that don't have at least one major feature built prior to 1800.
While compiling this book I have seen some incredible sights, like the wall painting of George and the Dragon on the external north wall at Aldingbourne, so faded that, like a ghost of its former self, it only appears in a certain light. I have also seen some beautiful scenery like Barlavington where the views are splendid and the silence is almost deafening. If this book can spark the interest of the reader to use it as it was meant to be used and visit these churches personally, he or she will not be disappointed, and I will have achieved my goal.

HOW TO USE THIS BOOK

Churches are grouped together in areas, the churches are listed from west to east in each area and their locations are indicated by the page number of the West Sussex 'A to Z' street atlas (WSSA).

Church ratings are in three categories:

❀ Picturesque settings and views

⌖ Interesting architectural or building features

📖 Historical or unusual interest

Ratings are from none to three of each.
Maps of each area appear at the start of each section.
There is a county map identifying the areas on page 9 and a typical church plan on page 142.

ABOUT THE AUTHOR

Paul Coppin was born in South London in 1950.In 1965 he joined the family business which he now runs. His interests have always been wide and varied; he was a semi-professional American football referee for thirteen years and is a keen collector of Goss heraldic china. He married his wife Janice in 1970 and has one daughter Charlotte. In 1999 he and his wife moved from London to a small hamlet just outside Lewes where they now live.

EARLY CHRISTIANITY IN SUSSEX

Christianity came late to Sussex, why was this? With the densely populated coastal strip less than fifty miles from London, and St Augustine's original Christian base of operations at Canterbury little more than sixty miles east, it would seem natural that the new religion would spread across the south before moving north. Truth is Sussex was a very different place in the seventh century than it is now. There was a major barrier between the far south and the rest of England and it was a natural one, the Andredes Weald. This was a forest so thick that virtually the only way to travel north overland was by following the river courses. The Romans had forced their straight roads through but even they had struggled, managing only a couple of main arterial roads reaching down to their supply ports on the south coast. In the centuries since the Romans quit Britain the forest had reclaimed much of the untended roads and that was just the way the South Saxons liked it, a defendable coastline in front and an impenetrable forest at their backs. In the second half of the first millennium if you visited the South Saxons in peace or war you came by sea. So with Christianity well established in the rest of England St Wilfrid came to Selsey by ship in 681 to convert the pagan Saxons.

The common belief is that Wilfrid set out on a religious crusade to bring the rest of the Saxon population into the Christian fold. Although undoubtedly a good and deeply religious man his main reason for coming was quite different. Wilfrid had been an important Bishop, Bishop of York, a highly influential diocese in an ecclesiastical hierarchy that was already showing the political aspirations that would reach their peak in the sixteenth century. Wilfrid had fallen into disfavour and at a meeting of the synod had been ordered to give up all his lands and incomes held in the name of the church. Using a political ploy still much in use today others of his faction suggested that he go somewhere well out of the limelight where he could still pursue his chosen work and when the time was right he could return to his former powerful position with perhaps some new success to his credit. Sounds familiar?

So with a group of very enthusiastic followers, some clearly full of religious fervour, some perhaps hoping for quick advancement by hanging on to the Bishop's vestment tails Wilfrid arrived near Selsey only to find almost at once he was not the first. Just a few miles down the road at Bosham an Irish monk called Dicuil and a handful of acolytes had been preaching the gospel for some time without a single convert. So why was Wilfrid successful almost from the very start when others had failed? I believe for three reasons, first he was an educated man with obvious public speaking, political and organisational skills from his days as Bishop. Second he chose his followers well, experienced missionaries who at once spread out into the countryside to establish 'minsters', bases of operation which included a church, many of which like Singleton survive today. Thirdly and most importantly he had backing. King Aethelwald, recently converted to Christianity in Wessex,welcomed him with open arms. A little later Caedwalla, either a Christian himself, or like King Ethelbert, St Augustine's patron in Kent, was married to one, started giving large tracts of land to Wilfrid for the building of churches and more importantly to provide the income to cover their upkeep.

Using the same method suggested to St Augustine by Pope Gregory sixty years before, churches were built on pagan religious sites and the congregation persuaded that the new religion was in fact just the correct version of their old beliefs. Dozens of Sussex churches sit on ancient earthworks (North Stoke), close to giant ancient yew trees long used as sacred pagan sites (Coldwaltham) or even as in the case of Bosham on the very foundations of a pre-Christian temple. The new religion suited the basically peaceful south Saxons much as it had their cousins in the north, both of whom, like the Normans who were to come in the second millennium, had integrated easily with the native population after a shaky start. As for Wilfrid he stayed close to his base in the Selsey area, directing the work and keeping a close eye on the situation in the rest of England through the busy port at Bosham. After only a few years his recall came. He left his Sussex ministry in good hands and returned to his former high position in the north with the conversion of the south Saxons as an ecclesiastical feather in his cap. Twice more he was to fall out with his fellow clerics and be deposed before his death in Northants in 709 aged 73. He was buried in Ripon where his shrine became a popular place of pilgrimage following his canonisation. Considered by many to be one of the most important men of the early English church his radical methods show up even in his will where he left part of his large fortune to his Abbots 'so that they might purchase the friendship of Kings and Bishops'.

As for Dicuil, the first known Christian missionary in Sussex, he is believed to have died in obscurity at Bosham and is possibly buried beneath the floor of his tiny church, the site of which is thought to be the crypt on the south side of the nave of Bosham church.

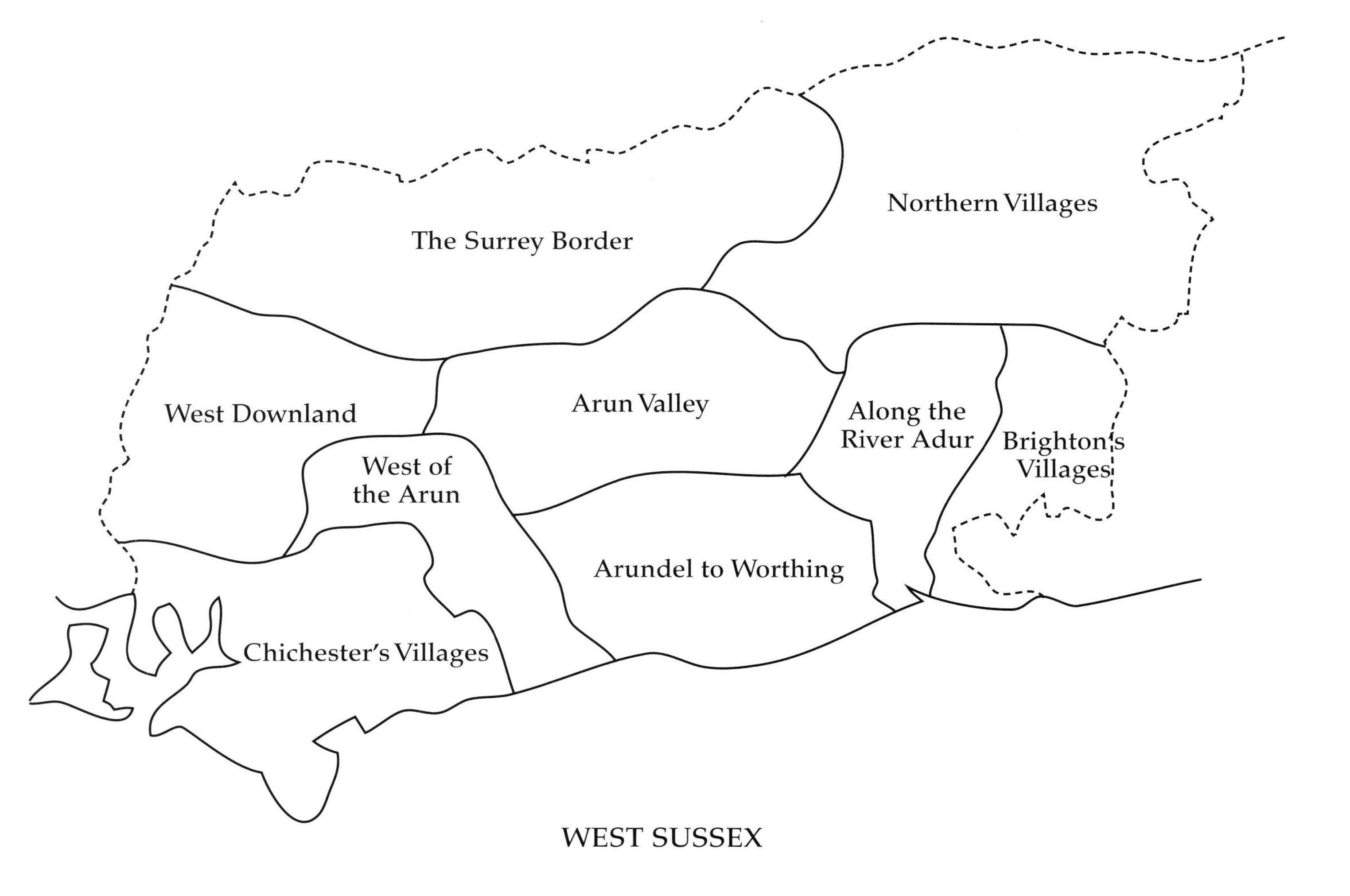
The Surrey Border
Northern Villages
West Downland
Arun Valley
Along the River Adur
Brighton's Villages
West of the Arun
Arundel to Worthing
Chichester's Villages
WEST SUSSEX

CHICHESTER'S VILLAGES

By the time St Wilfrid arrived in Selsey in 681AD the Roman town of Regnum (Chichester) was in ruins but the network of Roman roads leading from it were still usable. Using these roads the first Christian missionaries spread through the area to found some of the oldest churches in the county. Bosham was to become the most important church in Saxon Sussex. From Chidham St Cuthman would set out to spread the word northeast. In Norman times Boxgrove would become an important monastic house and Chichester would rise again to become the religious centre of the county.

WESTBOURNE *St John the Baptist* ❀ ✠✠ 📖📖📖 (WSSA)137

There are definite hints of an early Norman church at Westbourne but what stands today is mostly thirteenth century (aisle walling and part of chancel) fourteenth century (aisle windows, north vestry and west end of the nave) and early sixteenth century (three bay arcades and tower). The surviving fourteenth century perpendicular windows are good examples of their kind, the rest are modern replacements. The thirteenth century lancets in the chancel are now blocked but still show in the walls. The tower replaced an earlier version and now stands above the main body of the church on massive supports. The spire added in 1770 does nothing for the look of the church and the position of the clock face is more than a little odd. The French naval flag draped above the eastern tower support was captured in the West Indies in 1794 by Marine captain Thomas Oldfield who later served with Nelson at the Battle of the Nile and was killed in action at Acre in 1799. Memorials to many other Oldfields, some of them military men, are spread about the church. The church roof is mostly sixteenth century and looks in good condition. A beam now housed in the modern porch but originally from inside the church may be even older and is carved with the coats of arms of the Fitzalan Earls of Arundel. Two wall tablets in the chancel for the Barwell family (Henry d 1785, Richard d1804) are interesting in that they are so poorly made. There are a large number of ledger slabs set in the floor, mostly from the eighteenth century, some badly worn and many covered by seating. For me the church's real treasure is its churchyard. I have never seen such a large churchyard so crowded with interesting old stones. Gruesome carvings abound, skulls by the dozen, picks, spades and skeletons in every direction. There is even a stone carved with an open coffin showing a body inside. One fine stone for a farmer who lived into his eighties shows a wheat-sheaf and pitchfork to identify his trade. There are some very early chest tombs and two low tombs shaped like coffins. The avenue of yew trees that leads to the north door is spectacular and it is said that in the summer English sage still blooms amongst the stones. In medieval times this simple herb was often sown round tombstones as a symbol of immortality, the fact that it still grows back each year would suggest the reason why.

CHIDHAM *St Mary*   (WSSA)138

Situated on a peninsular that extends between Thorney Island and the formerly busy Saxon port at Bosham with its important church. Christianity must have come early to the area but of the early building nothing now remains. The present nave and part of the chancel are thirteenth century with the north aisle added about 100 years later. The north aisle end window is an interesting two-light lancet stepped to allow for the slope of the aisle roof. The only real addition since is the ugly bellcote built during the otherwise sympathetic restoration of 1864. This bell housing replaced a short clapboard bell turret, which is reported to have been more in keeping with the rest of the building. The bell turret was certainly in place as early as 1770 and had replaced a steeple that was recorded as 'in danger of collapse' in 1636. The font has proved difficult to date, some say Saxon others as late as 1660. Whatever the date it is an unusual ball shape and was found buried under the nave floor during the 1864 building work. Part of this restoration work involved enlarging the chancel arch to its present size using the original stones where possible. The square opening in the north nave wall led to the former rood loft in medieval times. The aisle pillars with their typical pointed arches of the period show signs of pilgrim graffiti. This would come from the time when the church was a popular destination for pilgrims visiting the shrine of St Cuthman who was born in Chidham and lived there before his famous journey to Steyning (see Steyning church). The church must have been quite rich at that time but following the Reformation, with pilgrimages stopped by order of the king, the church fell into disrepair. A string of poor quality vicars did not help matters, one was brought before the ecclesiastical court for drunkenness, another was 'of poor education'. By 1770 a good rector was in place and the church described as 'in good order'. The two excellent marble wall plaques in the chancel date from early in Queen Anne's reign (1707 and 1708) and are believed to be the work of a London sculptor. One has two large skulls at the bottom; this kind of gruesome symbol was in fashion in the eighteenth century and is often seen on gravestones of the same era. One or two of these old stones can be found in the lightly populated churchyard, which is well cared for.

WEST ITCHENOR *St Nicholas* ❀❀ ⌖ 📖 (WSSA)160

The single cell church of St Nicholas stands close to the water of Chichester harbour and has changed little since it was built in the early thirteenth century. There is a good fifteenth century window in the south nave wall and a modern rebuild of a similar window opposite but the rest are for the most part undisturbed lancets contemporary with the building of the church. The church has a great deal of good stained glass some of it very modern in style (west wall). At night the church is cleverly lit to show off its stained glass. The thirteenth century font is smaller than usual and is particularly interesting in that the base and font fit together to give the impression of being all one piece. Fonts of this date are quite rare in Sussex. Almost all the interior fittings of the church are modern with only the gallery being of particular interest. Still serving a gallery's original purpose as a music centre it is also the church's war memorial. There is a fine ledger slab in the chancel floor dated 1780 inscribed for the wife of Murdoch Mackenzie, Royal Navy. MacKenzie was the navy hydrographer who charted Chichester harbour in the 1780s, a copy of his chart is on show in the vestry. The entrance to the church is still the original south doorway, the Norman north door although now blocked can still be seen in the nave wall. There are three bells in the bellcote, two are seventeenth century, the third (the treble) was made in 1530 by John White of Reading and is considered especially noteworthy. The one-piece wooden chiming wheels were disconnected in 1989 but due to their unusual early design are preserved in the bellcote. The porch is modern but the stones that make up its floor are old, mostly eighteenth century grave stones from the churchyard, but there are also two thirteenth century coffin slabs, one with an intricate cross carved into it. These slabs and two others to be found in the churchyard would originally have been inside the church slightly protruding from the earth floor. In the churchyard there are a few old stones still standing and many more have been used to make a path to the north of the church. There is now a strong boundary wall but this was not always the case. In medieval times few churchyards were fenced. One possible reason for the change can be found in the West Itchenor church records of 1621 when the churchyard was described as 'open to all beasts, hereby the graves are rooted up, to the grief of the parishioners'.

WEST WITTERING *St Peter & St Paul* ❀ ⊕⊕ 📖📖 (WSSA)176

Land was given for the building of a church here in 740AD and from that church survives the gable cornerstone on show in a case in the nave. The stone is carved with a cross on both sides and it is believed it was used in three different churches on the same site. The large plain font may date from the second Saxon church. If so, it is in remarkable condition. Much of the present nave is part of the Norman church built 1150; its south aisle was added in 1180. Between 1220 and 1260 a massive rebuilding programme was instigated, perhaps by St Richard (Bishop of Chichester 1245-53) who was a parishioner of Wittering and took a close interest in its church. The aisle was pushed east to form a chapel, but was soon knocked through into the chancel, which was rebuilt along with its arch. The tower is also from this period. (A massive thirteenth century wooden ladder is used to reach the bells, which are housed in a huge wooden cage). Both north and south doorways are very late thirteenth century, the north one has pilgrim crosses scratched in to its jamb, many more can be seen in the side chapel. Although damaged, the two wall tombs in north wall of the chancel are considered important examples of their kind. Both are early sixteenth century and made for the Ernley family. The church's most intriguing treasure is a stone lid carved with a cross and Bishop's staff. Too small to be a coffin lid it was found upside down in the chancel floor being used as a paving slab. It is now believed to be the lid of a reliquary which perhaps stood in the recess still to be seen in the east wall of the side chapel. We will never know which saint's bones it held, but St Richard would seem likely. Canonised in 1252 it is known for certain that St Richard's bones were divided between several churches. There are some stones of interest in the churchyard including one with a carving of a ship for a drowned sailor erected by his captain who is himself buried nearby. Land bequeathed to the church in 1633 is still providing 8 to 20 bushels of wheat for the poor almost 400 years later.

BOSHAM *Holy trinity* ❀❀❀ ✠✠✠ 📖📖📖 (WSSA)138

When St Wilfrid arrived at nearby Selsey in 680 to introduce Christianity to Sussex he was surprised to find an Irish monk called Dicuil had already established a church at Bosham on the ruins of a Roman basilica. The nearby natural harbour grew to become a major port in Saxon times and it was from here that King Harold sailed to Normandy to stake his claim to the English throne and the church is clearly depicted and named in the Bayeux tapestry. King Canute had a home here in the tenth century, legend says that his eight-year-old daughter was drowned in the stream behind the church and was buried in the nave. A stone coffin of the correct age found under the chancel arch during nineteenth century restoration did indeed contain the body of a female child of about eight years. The very scale of the church indicates its importance and wealth. The Domesday Book shows Bosham to be one of the richest endowments in England in 1086. The tower, with its one remaining Saxon window and interesting corbel table, was built along with the nave and westernmost part of the chancel in 800AD. The chancel was enlarged about 1040 when the spectacular chancel arch was built and was again pushed east in 1300. North and south aisles were added at this time causing the loss of the Saxon nave walls. The chancel arch, which looks as if it deserves to be unique, is in fact the same as the one at nearby Stoughton, both probably built by the same mason. In 1865 the chancel roof was raised to its original pre-fifteenth century height uncovering a fine set of corbels in the shape of human heads (one probably the likeness of the master mason that made them). The pointed opening looking down into the nave from the tower was a door to a former nave upper storey room, note the tiny window next to it. The fourteenth century south doorway still has its original nail-studded door on the inside and there are crosses scratched by crusaders on its jamb. Standing a little above (and reaching considerably below) the south aisle is a crypt thought to be the site of Dicuil's first church and was used as a charnel house for the Benedictine monks who followed him.

BIRDHAM *St James* ❀ ✝✝ 📖📖 (WSSA)161

The earliest recorded mention of a church at Birdham is 1105 but of that building nothing remains. The present church is, with the exception of the 1882 chancel, substantially fourteenth century. Both north and south doorways, the tower base and much of the roof are of this date, as are the tower and chancel arches. The chancel arch of two orders is a particularly good example of the gothic architecture of that period. The roof is not only old but also complex, it has three tie beams with two king posts as supports and there are four sets of brackets that form part of the wall plates. The tower was rebuilt in the sixteenth century when its height was lowered; the fourteenth century bell frame was reused in the new tower and is still in use today. One of the two bells is also fourteenth century and is inscribed 'Johannes', the other is dated 1695. Much of the church interior was replaced when the chancel was rebuilt and the musician's gallery was dismantled in 1882. There is a rare fourteenth century tile on show bearing the coat of arms of the St John family who were benefactors of the church at that time. The south porch was built in 1545 but has seen considerable refurbishment since then. Most churches have buttresses that are later additions. At Birdham they are all contemporary with the building of the nave except those on the tower, the one on the south side second from the west and its opposite number to the north. There are some interesting eighteenth century stones in the churchyard and a strange twisted tree. This is a macrocarpa tree believed to be over 200 years old.

APULDRAM *St Mary the Virgin* ❀❀ ✠✠ 📖 (WSSA)161

Built as a chapel of ease for Bosham in the twelfth century there is no village nearby and never was. A long narrow footpath leads to the church and then carries on to the shore of one arm of Chichester harbour. Stonework from the first chapel can still be seen in the nave walls of the largely thirteenth century church that exists today. The chancel is a particularly fine example of Early English architecture with no expense spared in its building. There are a set of three typical lancet windows in each of the three chancel walls and all nine windows are set in decorative arcading; there is also a canopied piscina and rare fourteenth century floor tiles close to the altar. There is no arch to divide the nave and chancel but a good late fourteenth century screen serves in its place. The ancient coffin lid with carved cross is contemporary with the chancel. There is a squint in the east respond of the nave arcade and this too is ornately decorated. The stairs that once led to the rood loft remain in the north wall. The font is Norman and is decorated with shallow arcades. In the fifteenth century porch is an unusual mass dial scratched on the eastern windowsill, whoever scratched it was clever enough to use the jamb as the gnomon that marks the sun's passage. The bellcote has provision for three bells but there are now only two, these are chimed with wooden hammers. Both bells have been recast, the treble because it cracked as a result of concussion caused by the firing of rifles at a naval funeral. The church sits in a peaceful and picturesque setting with some old grave markers of interest including a couple of unusual intricate iron ones.

SELSEY *St Wilfrid & St Peter* ❀ ✢ 📖📖 (WSSA)179

The medieval parish church of Selsey must surely be one of the oddest in England, being as it is divided into two halves and standing in two different places. In 1866 it was decided to move the parish church from its isolated site at Church Norton into the town of Selsey but church law prohibits the moving of a chancel to a new site, so only the nave was dismantled and rebuilt to form part of St Peter's, Selsey. The Chancel at Church Norton, now a chapel dedicated to St Wilfrid, dates from the twelfth century but most of what we see today is thirteenth century with a few late medieval additions The old chancel arch can clearly be seen as part of the west wall. Inside there is a fine sixteenth century canopy tomb to John Lewis and his wife and the floor is lined with some ancient coffin slabs. The mound near the church was probably a Saxon fort. It has yielded artefacts from Roman and Saxon times and there is evidence that St Wilfrid, the bringer of Christianity to Sussex, who arrived in this area in the late seventh century built his main church where the chapel now stands. A stone 'palm cross' made in St Wilfrid's time stood in the churchyard and is believed to have been similar to the one he constructed at Bewcastle. It was destroyed during the reformation but a few stones from the original have been incorporated into the copy that forms the war memorial at St Peter's. The chapel now serves a useful life as the chapel for the town cemetery, in the middle of which it stands. The old stones from the churchyard have been moved to the boundary wall. One or two services are still held at the chapel, most notably on St Wilfrid's day (12th Oct). Two miles away at St Peter's the rebuilt nave contains interesting pillars and the old roof from Church Norton. The font is early Norman and large enough for the total immersion which was still in fashion at that time. The church is famous for its lectern which some say is pre-Reformation. For some reason not recorded when St Peter's was built the usual east-west alignment was shifted by 90 degrees so that what would have been the east window faces north, just one more oddity of this 'church of two halves'.

EAST LAVANT *St Mary* ❀ ✠ 📖 (WSSA)120

This unusual looking church has its roots in the twelfth century but the only visual remains of any substance from that period is the west wall. Both of the nave walls were lost to aisles in the thirteenth century but of those aisles only the middle arches of the south arcade remain. The church's two best features are the Norman west doorway with recessed shafts (known as 'nook shafts') and a fine round arch with chevron decoration, and the brick tower of 1671. Inside the tower is a plaque detailing its building and a fourteenth century tomb re-sited from the old chancel where it probably served as the Easter sepulchre. There are two coffin slabs in the floor of the north aisle, these probably date from the thirteenth century, and one carries an inscription in Norman French. The royal coats of arms are those of the Stuart Kings and are not often seen in Sussex churches. Five early sixteenth century stalls, with plain misericords, survive in the Victorian chancel. Gordon Hills, one of the most unsympathetic and energetic church architects of the Victorian age, carried out the restoration of 1863. He was responsible for the loss of many unique and irreplaceable features from the thirty Sussex churches he descended upon in the nineteenth century, his only saving grace is that some churches may have fallen down completely had he not intervened. All the really old stones in the churchyard seem to have been removed and used as paving stones for the paths. I have seen this done before and it does not always work, but here it is well done; note especially the three steps on the west side made from large tomb slabs. The setting is quite impressive with the church sitting on high ground with the Lavant stream passing nearby.

WESTHAMPNETT *St Peter* ❀ ✠✠✠ 📖 (WSSA)140

The church is built very close to the old Roman 'Stane Street' on a Saxon diversion that looped round an area of the untended stone road that had become unusable. Much of the chancel is Saxon and a large amount of the building material is made up of pre-used items looted from the ruined Roman town of Regnum (now modern Chichester). Tiles, bricks, faced stone cut on the Isle of Wight and even hollow hypocaust pipes can clearly be seen, some with the Roman makers marks still visible. Regnum was uninhabited and being looted for stone about 710AD which would be a clue to the building date of the early church. This would make St Peter's one of the oldest surviving churches in Sussex being built just thirty years after St Wilfrid landed at Selsey. Also on the south side is a blocked Saxon window and some typical Saxon 'herringbone' stonework. The chancel was partly re-built in the thirteenth century and has a pronounced inclination to the south. Pictures survive of the Saxon chancel arch which although known at the time to have been unique was destroyed in 1867. In the chancel the Sackville tomb which was badly damaged by Cromwellian soldiers during the Civil War, serves as the Easter sepulchre. The present nave was built in 1200 and is a good example of the transitional style that links the Norman and Early English architectural periods. On the sill of the low side window many crudely carved pilgrim signs can still be seen. These signs whose meanings have mostly been lost are often found in churches on roads used by pilgrims. So popular was this church as a stopping place a papal decree was issued granting the selling of indulgences to pilgrims who stopped to pray there. Close to the porch doorjamb a simple cross is cut into the stonework. This was possibly one of several 'consecration crosses', used when the building was first consecrated. The font is sixteenth century, a rare date for a font. One of the three bells is dated 1581 and another 1632. Made by the stained glass makers Clayton and Bell the east window is considered the best of all their many Sussex church windows. Three Bishops of Chichester rest in the churchyard along with many of the English cricketing family, the Lillywhites.

MERSTON *St Giles* ⊕ (WSSA)163

The church setting is spoilt by the ugly building of indeterminate use that all but blocks the entrance to the churchyard. Although the church appears to be a single cell building the divide between chancel and nave is clear from the outside at least. Both nave and chancel ends are thirteenth century and the north aisle is of much the same date. The roof forms a single span over both sides, sweeping so low on the north side to cover the aisle that no room is left for any windows, although a door is squeezed in. On the south side are three lancets, all slightly different but of much the same date. The west window, in the perpendicular style, is fifteenth century but the east window is modern. The main door is on the south side protected by a brick porch with a tie beam dated 1637. The font is twelfth century and looks to have had the top few inches removed, probably to level off the wear. This has left incomplete arcading on its sides. The uneven churchyard contains a few old stones and tombs but none of any particular interest. The present bell housing replaced a wooden bellcote, probably early in the nineteenth century as the present bell is dated 1807.

TANGMERE *St Andrew*   (WSSA)141

From the old pre-Conquest Saxon church fragments of stonework survive, notably in the nave walls which are for the most part early twelfth century and contain a few re-used Roman bricks. At the south end of the nave there are four early Norman windows (two each side) the most easterly one on the south side has a re-used decorated Saxon stone as its headstone. It is badly worn and is thought to show the beheading of John the Baptist although the two-legged figures appear to have animal heads, a form of symbolism not unknown in Saxon carvings. Also of great age is the tub-shaped font, believed to be one of the oldest in Sussex. The chancel was re-built and extended in the thirteenth century and the wide lancets that form the east window are from that time. Almost all the other windows are modern replacements. The bell turret is supported by a massive oak frame in the nave, and contains three bells. The oldest was made by the itinerant bellfounder John Cole (see Findon church) about 1590 and is probably the last bell he made in Sussex before moving to Kent. Tangmere is an old village mentioned in the grants of land made by King Caedwalla to St Wilfrid in the seventh century and it has seen much of our history, not the least of which was during the Second World War. Tangmere was a major RAF airbase during the Battle of Britain in 1940 and because of its proximity to the coast and the European mainland, stayed on a war footing later than many other airfields. The churchyard bears witness to this with the graves of many young airmen, British, Allied and even German who died in the surrounding area fighting for their respective countries. At the time of writing the church was undergoing major refurbishment, the effect of which remains to be seen, but with the more enlightened views of modern church restoration and the laws protecting historic buildings I suspect the end result will be a return to its former glory.

BOXGROVE *St Mary & St Blaise* ❀❀❀ ✠✠✠ 🕮🕮 (WSSA)141

The original priory at Boxgrove was constructed in 1117 and expanded steadily until its demise in 1536 during the Dissolution of the Monasteries. What remains today as the parish church consists of the priory chancel, transepts, tower and the former choir now the church nave. The five-bay nave of 1220 was demolished as surplus to requirements and its ruins can still be seen to the west of the church. The oldest parts surviving are the transepts, built about 1120. In the north, signs of the monks' night stairs can still be seen. In the south transept, now the chapel of St Blaise, a statue of the saint stands on an original wooden plinth. The chancel is untouched thirteenth century and truly magnificent with three tall lancet windows containing good Victorian stained glass. Some thirteenth century floor tiles survive on the south side of the chancel. Both chancel and present nave have vaulted stone ceilings, these were beautifully painted in the sixteenth century by Lambert Barnard. Two chapels stand either side of the chancel, St Catherine to the north and St John to the south. Both contain ancient stone altar slabs one of which was recovered from the churchyard. The large tower above the crossing was built about 1170 and contains two seventeenth century bells (one, at least, has been re-cast), which replaced former bells destroyed by lightning. Perhaps the church's greatest benefactor was Thomas de la Warr who was responsible for many of the church's unique features like the painted ceiling and his most important addition the de la Warr chantry chapel. This chapel built in 1534 is free-standing and has been described as a church within a church. It is ornately decorated and has its own vaulted roof. Completed just before Henry VIII dissolved the monasteries, permission was never granted for the de la Warrs to be buried there and it was never used as a tomb. There are several canopied wall tombs and chest tombs in the aisles, most of which carry no markings. The fifteenth century carved font must have once stood in the nave of the priory and been moved to its present position at a later time. A model of the priory as it was in 1534 is on show inside the church. A walk around the churchyard and a look at the ruined nave and nearby ruined priory guesthouse is a must.

ALDINGBOURNE *St Mary* ❀ ✠✠ 📖📖 (WSSA)142

A Saxon church of some importance at Aldingbourne is mentioned in the Domesday Book and from it part of the north and west walls may still exist, but for the most part today's church is twelfth and thirteenth century.A fine Norman south doorway is protected by a seventeenth century porch and has a few crusader crosses scratched into its jamb. The chancel and south aisle are twelfth century and the latter has interesting columns and traces of wall paintings. The north aisle has gone and all the arches of the arcade were blocked centuries ago. When the vestry was built the westernmost arch was opened up to give access and decorative geometric wall paintings were discovered in near perfect condition. Dated at 1180 they may be the oldest church wall paintings in Sussex. One can only imagine what awaits discovery if the other arches are ever opened up. The tower was built in the thirteenth century but there is evidence that it may have partially collapsed around 1500. The lower portions and west door are certainly original but there are several grants of money dated 1536 for'building the new tower at Aldingbourne'. There are several good ledger slabs on the floor as well as a medieval stone coffin lid. There are two fonts, one is dated 1180 made of polished Sussex marble, the other is much older and crudely made. It is believed to have come from the seventh century monastery of Lidsey. On the west wall survives a rare painted consecration cross, the external carved ones often survive(five can be seen on the old altar slab behind the present altar) but the painted ones are very rare. The royal coats of arms on the south wall are those of William III. The original dedication of the church is unknown but it is my personal belief that it was St George. The excellent south chapel with vaulted roof contains the latest in a long line of statues of St George. The cult of St George was brought back from the east by crusaders who are known to have had links with the church. Finally, and most intriguingly, if you stand outside the church looking at what is now the external north wall, but was once the internal north aisle wall, a painting of St George killing the dragon can sometimes be seen in certain light conditions.

BARNHAM *St Mary* ❀ ✠✠ 📖📖 (WSSA)143

The church stood close to a tidal creek in Saxon times and the local industry was fishing, with a little smuggling in later years. Artefacts found nearby strongly hint at a Saxon church on the site but the nave standing today is from the first Norman church of about 1100. The south wall and doorway remain untouched but the north wall was pierced in 1300 to create a north aisle. This aisle was removed in the early sixteenth century but the remains of its arches can still be seen both inside and out. One arch does remain intact and forms the entrance to the modern vestry. All of the walls were at one time painted with red/brown wash and this still shows up clearly, on the south wall this looks quite attractive contrasting as it does with the white edge stones of the splayed windows. The chancel arch is made of plaster and braced wooden struts forming a tympanum. Early in the thirteenth century the old chancel was removed and a much larger version built. The south windows with their central lozenge are interesting, they are of a crude tracery design that was soon to develop into the delicate Decorated style (1290-1350). The damaged square font is contemporary with the nave and has some pilgrim crosses scratched on the side. In the passage leading to the vestry is more ancient graffiti protected by a glass cover. These include the usual crosses and other Christian symbols, some with meanings lost in time, but the most interesting is a Latin inscription. Crudely carved by a passing pilgrim it translates as 'Pray for my father who died at Agincourt'. The bell weighs over 150 Kg, was cast in 1348 and is one of the oldest in the county. Although the fine wooden statue of St Elizabeth of Hungary came to the church in the twentieth century, it was made in the low countries around 1380 and gives us some idea of the statues that would have adorned the rood beam in most churches in medieval times. There is a horse-drawn plough on show in the nave. The restored brick porch is thirteenth century and a very early example of its kind. Close to the church are some old grave markers and the churchyard in general is interesting. Note its steep stepped access in one corner.

CHURCH FONTS

Surveys show that more tourists visit churches to see the font than for any other reason. Perhaps this is because, whereas the church is always changing, the font usually stays almost unchanged. More often than not the font is the oldest feature in the building. It is also the most personal thing in the church, marking the religious beginning of thousands of local people's passage through life. Some fonts have had hundreds of tiny crosses roughly scratched on their sides by proud parents, Beddingham (East Sussex) is the best example.

The font is usually positioned at the back of the church close to the central aisle symbolically marking the start of life's journey towards God's altar at the other end of the aisle. A door is also close by, left open during the baptism to allow the devil to leave when the subject is 'cleansed' by the holy water from the font.

Every county in the land seems to have some aspect of their fonts unique to that area, in Sussex it's the large number of ancient fonts and a building material virtually unknown outside the county, Sussex Marble. Sussex marble is a stone formed by layers of sea sediment often with a greenish hue. Although sometimes seen rough cut it is at its best when polished to reveal the shells of tiny sea creatures trapped in the sediment. The stone was used in Sussex for centuries, the best coming from the Kirdford area, but was quarried out in the late nineteenth century and is now no longer available in usable quantities.

Because of its remoteness in the past Sussex has retained a large number of truly ancient fonts including several Saxon ones, notably at Poling, Bepton, Tangmere and Ford and there are so many Norman fonts that they are commonplace. Early fonts were large and set low to the ground for immersion was the fashion. Adults would stand in the font and the water would be poured over them, infants were totally immersed. The font at Selham is certainly from this period. This is also why so many early fonts now stand on later plinths, added to raise their height. Poling and Slaugham are good examples.

Saxon fonts were usually bowl or tub shaped (Tangmere) and early Norman fonts round (Chithurst) or square (Coates) but by the end of the thirteenth cent almost all fonts being made were octagonal. Many older square fonts were altered to the new shape, Stopham may be an example.

In the fourteenth century total immersion was out of fashion and fonts were being made smaller and the heavy carvings of the Norman period had given way to more delicate decoration. A century later font architecture had reached its peak with ornate decoration of every kind from fish (Slaugham) to royal rosettes(Burpham). Sussex is perhaps lacking in fonts from this golden age of fonts, as few were needed in Sussex at that time, Boxgrove is a rare exception.

Following the Reformation in the sixteenth century there seems to have been a feeling that the font was tied in with Popish ceremony and many fonts were destroyed, so much so that Elizabeth I had to issue a proclamation stating that fonts should not be removed from churches. Westhampnett has a font made in the sixteenth century.

Worse was to come during Cromwell's commonwealth when the use of fonts was banned. The puritan influence led to the destruction of hundreds of fonts especially those made entirely of lead, these were often melted down to make musket balls for the army. At Pyecombe the lead font was painted white to hide the valuable lead from sight. Only about thirty-five lead fonts survive in England and West Sussex has three, one of the best in the land is the one at Pyecombe made from a single sheet of lead with no visible joins. The other two are at Edburton and Parham. Many stone fonts were thrown into the churchyard only to be reinstated centuries later (Steyning), or hidden by the priests sometimes to be forgotten for hundreds of years. The font at Chidham was found under the nave floor, Ford's was reclaimed from a farmyard where it was used as a drinking trough. Some were vandalised by Roundhead soldiers, at Cuckfield the font is cracked, the result of being kicked by a cavalry horse stabled in the church during the Civil War.

By 1662 a king once again ruled England, the font was back in favour and many replacements were needed, the font at Warminghurst is from this time. At Lurgashall the font was broken by puritans then repaired in 1662 and reinstated on Lady Day of that year. Fonts from the seventeenth century appear to be rush jobs and are rarely of good quality. At Udimore in East Sussex there is a seventeenth century wooden font painted to look like stone. This was probably a quick and cheap temporary replacement.

Few fonts were needed in the eighteenth century so they are a rare find, the author is unaware of any in West Sussex.

In the nineteenth century Victorian restoration destroyed many ancient features in churches and fonts were not spared, many once again found their way into the churchyard only to be reclaimed in recent years, some were lost for ever.

Some Sussex fonts are well over one thousand years old, they are not in museums showing what things were like in ages past. They are still performing their original task, week in week out, year in year out and there is absolutely no reason why they should not continue to do so for another thousand years. It is little wonder therefore that they hold the interest of so many people today.

WEST DOWNLAND

Close to the Hampshire border this area has a rich and varied mix of churches. Saxon Stoughton and impressive Harting were important churches in their day, Trotton and Bepton are full of interest. All are in picturesque settings but especially the three Mardens.

SOUTH HARTING *St Mary & St Gabriel* ❀ ✠ ✠ (WSSA)78

This church, by far the largest in the area, sits on high ground and looks straight down the village high street. Cruciform in shape it is for the most part fourteenth century with substantial Victorian restoration. On the south side is the ruined chapel of the Caryll family, the tombs from the chapel were moved into the church during restoration work after years exposed to the weather. The church has been struck by lightning several times and following a fire caused by one of these strikes in 1576 new aisle and tower arches were needed as well as new roofs in all areas. The three common types of church roof can all be seen from the crossing at Harting. King post in the nave, trussed rafter in the transepts and a complex arrangement of tie and collar beams in the chancel. Although not old (1848) the newel staircase to the tower is worthy of note, built and designed by a local craftsman it squeezes itself into a very small area and is a work of art. The font is thirteenth century as is the rare figure of the Virgin Mary in the south transept. High on the south wall of the nave at the east end is a piscina, this once served an altar in the rood loft. The churchyard is well kept and contains some interesting stones. The war memorial is particularly well done in a kind of modern Celtic style. Unlike most spires in the county, which are shingled, this one was covered in copper in the eighteenth century giving the church a very distinctive look.

RACTON *St Peter* ❀ ✠✠ 📖📖 (WSSA)117

The church at Racton certainly existed in 1142 when the lord of the manor gave the church to Lewes Priory. Most of the walls are from the twelfth century church, with additions and refurbishment in the thirteenth. The west wall was completely re-built within the next hundred years and the west door and window date from that re-build. The south doorway is late eighteenth century but the wooden door is ancient and still retains its original metalwork. The simple font is twelfth century but much restored. The nave roof is an ancient trussed rafter type and very low. A good description of this church would be 'cosy'; not a word often used to describe a church. There is no chancel arch and a large tie beam supporting the royal arms of George II acts as the divide between the chancel and nave. The chancel east window was changed to its present perpendicular shape in the fifteenth century. The aumbry and piscina are thirteenth century, as is the lancet window in the south wall. Also in the south wall are a square headed two-light window and priest's door from the fifteenth century. To the left of the altar are three interesting memorials. The oldest is the table tomb of John Gunter (d1557), closer to the east wall is the wall tomb of Sir George Gunter (d1624) and his wife. This tomb, which shows two kneeling figures, was repainted in recent years while the original colours were still visible to use as a guide. In between the two is an excellent bust of Sir Charles Nicholl (d1733) with funeral armour hanging above. It was fashionable at one time for knights to have armour specially made to be carried at their funeral and then hung in the church, there are many examples in Sussex. The churchyard is an uneven shape and contains few stones. The church stands close to the road but in a pleasant setting with an old cottage close by said to have lodged Charles II on his way to exile in France. There is some backing for this claim as it was Racton lord of the manor Colonel George Gunter who organised the king's escape from Brighton.

CHITHURST *St Mary* ❀❀❀ ✠✠ 📖 (WSSA)57

Never a big parish (Domesday Book lists it as '6 villagers, 3 small holders, 3 slaves, a small church and a mill. Total value 60 shillings). Chithurst has never needed a large church so the charming plain church with simple lines has remained almost unchanged since it was built in late Saxon or very early Norman times. From its heyday of sixteen families in 1724 the congregation had by 1956 dwindled to one person attending the one service held per month and the building was in danger of being closed and demolished. The church was saved by re-organisation of local parish boundaries and became the chapel of Trotton church. The Sunday service held once every three weeks is once again well attended, but above all it has become a place for quiet meditation and contemplation.
Built on a pagan mound just yards from the rushing waters of the River Rother the setting is near perfect and those visiting the excellent church at nearby Trotton are well advised to add Chithurst to their tour. The only major changes to the original building are the west door, porch and south window, all fourteenth century, and the thirteenth century two-light east window. Inside the church is very plain with a narrow Norman chancel arch with a somewhat later squint on its north side. The bowl-shaped early Norman font has probably stood in its present position for over nine hundred years, its ornate cover spoils the font's simple lines somewhat. The piscina in the chancel was added in the thirteenth century. There is only one memorial in the church proper plus two worn slabs on the floor of the porch in memory of the Bettesworth family. The pews on the south side are sixteenth century, the others later copies. The list of rectors shows that the Rev John Denham was murdered in 1757 while returning from Stedham, a man named Aps was arrested for the deed, tried at Horsham and hanged. The very pleasant churchyard contains some old stones, some with gruesome carvings but the most interesting markers are the stone slabs that form a line next to the path close to the church wall. These are ancient and probably not in their original positions. They could well be Saxon and were almost certainly coffin lids protruding from the earth floor in the nave. Note how the moss growing on these lids has enhanced the designs carved on them.

UP MARDEN *St Michael* ❀❀ ✠✠ 📖 (WSSA)98

Like many churches dedicated to St Michael the church sits on high ground and looks down onto East and North Marden churches in the downland valley below. Almost totally un-restored and still lit by candles the church gives a good impression of what a church was like in the thirteenth century, when it was built. Still with its original lancet windows and three entrances the building has changed little in 700 years. The west door, once the main entrance, now opens into the low tower added in the early fourteenth century and capped with a bell turret, now too weak to hold the bells. All three of the bells are seventeenth century, two of which are dated 1620 and 1624. One is now hung close to the south porch the others are on the rough brick floor of the nave. There are remains of early wall paintings, in poor condition but considered important examples due to their odd composition and style. The most striking feature inside the building is the chancel arch. The narrow very pointed arch is sixteenth century, hurriedly inserted to protect the collapsing Early English arch still visible in the plaster surround. The painted tie beams of the nave roof are supported by wall plates with typical Norman style mouldings. All told a particularly pleasant interior to a rarely used shepherd's church, which has always served a widely spread community of farms rather than a village. Outside, the church appears to be in poor state of repair, the porch particularly so, but restoration of at least the porch is in hand. I have in the past seen churchyards being reclaimed by the ancient yew trees that often pre-date the church and Up Marden is a good example. Many grave markers are lost in the thick undergrowth as the trees try to reassert their pre-Christian domination.

Retired stones, East Lavant

Late sun picks out the inscription, Slaugham

Path edged with old stones, Walberton

Gruesome 18th century gravestone, Ardingly

'Leaping boards', Slaugham

Wooden grave boards, Twineham

1000 year-old font, Yapton

Lead font, Edburton

NORTH MARDEN *St Mary* ❀ ⌖⌖⌖ 🕮 (WSSA)98

This tiny church next to a farmyard at the end of an unmade road is one of only three in England to retain its single cell apsidal format unchanged. Built in 1130 all of the walls and one window (west wall above the modern window) are original. All the other windows are modern replacements but done in the Norman style, even to the use of Caen stone. Setting aside the apse, of which only five survive in Sussex, the church's best feature is the Norman south doorway. With mouldings elaborately carved in several Norman styles it is made from Caen stone which must have been brought at great expense and hardship across the channel, to either Chichester or Bosham, and hauled up to the site by pack horse or cart. The inside of the doorway is higher but plainer than the outside. The church interior is quite plain, with no division between nave and chancel, and there are few memorials. There is a full set of the nineteenth century prayer boards that were compulsory at the time. These list the Ten Commandments, the Creed and the Lord's Prayer. The small royal coat of arms is unusual, being fashioned in iron. The sandstone font is twelfth century on a fourteenth century base. The porch and north vestry are modern and the bellcote Victorian, other than that the building is basically unchanged in nine hundred years. The churchyard contains just ten stones, the oldest readable one is dated 1776.

EAST MARDEN *St Peter*  ⊕  (WSSA)98

The simple single cell church of St Peter's sits high up in the centre of the tiny village of East Marden. The western nave part is twelfth century with the chancel end being rebuilt in the thirteenth century, perhaps to square off an apse shape similar to the one at North Marden. Although there is no architectural divide between the chancel and nave,the chancel is defined by being completely wood panelled, including the roof. There are seven ancient tie beams in the roof, two in the chancel area and five in the nave. Two of the nave beams support the bellcote that contains one bell (probably nineteenth century) which replaced the two bells known to have been there in 1770. The chancel windows are thirteenth century, with original stonework on the inside but modern work outside. The lancet in the north wall of the nave is thirteenth century as is the north doorway, which now leads to the vestry. The goblet-shaped font with decorative lead lining is twelfth century but sits on a modern base. The large memorial slabs on the chancel walls are all eighteenth century and were, I suspect, floor slabs in the past. The organ is of some historical interest, it was formerly owned and played by Prince Albert, husband to Queen Victoria. The main door is protected by a seventeenth century brick porch. The fine cockerel-shaped weather vane seems fitting for this simple church in a picturesque rural setting.

ELSTED *St Paul* ❀ ✠✠ 📖 (WSSA)78

All of the nave walls with the exception of the south are eleventh century and contain arguably the best herringbone masonry in Sussex. The chancel arch and the blocked arches of the former north aisle are twelfth century but the chancel was rebuilt in the thirteenth. The chancel has a simple but effective two light lancet east window typical of the Early English period and similar single lancets in its north and south walls. The church fell into disrepair around 1730, this was allowed to continue until the mid-nineteenth century when the church was abandoned in favour of a new church at nearby Treyford. In 1893 a falling tree destroyed the nave roof and south wall and all but the chancel was open to the elements until the middle of the twentieth century. In 1951 the church at Treyford was blown up having failed to stand the test of time and the church at Elsted was rebuilt in a very sympathetic way bringing together the old and the new to form the pleasant church we see today. The church was re-dedicated in 1951.

STOUGHTON *St Mary* ❀ ✠✠✠ 📖 (WSSA)118

This important church was built almost entirely in the mid-eleventh century with only the smallest of additions since. Some books describe it as Norman but if this is so then the builders were working entirely to Saxon methods and that seems unlikely. All the Saxon trademarks are there, tall thin walls with high windows, long and short work on all corners, herringbone stonework; it has to be Saxon, about 1050 in my view. The magnificent chancel arch adds weight to this date, being almost the twin of the arch at Bosham. All of the windows were 'modernised' in the thirteenth and fourteenth centuries and the arches to the transepts are from this same period but rest on much older jambs. These side chapels are much like 'Porticus', a style of Saxon chapel that developed into tower building in later years. Indeed here the fourteenth century bell tower sits above the south Porticus supported by a massive timber frame. An ancient oak bell frame holds three of the five bells (two sixteenth, one fourteenth century). The west door and south chancel priest's door again have thirteenth century exteriors but are older on the inside. The chancel had its roof lowered by a metre or two in the late sixteenth century, cutting the top off the south window. It never ceases to amaze me how skilful medieval builders were, often better than those who were to follow. A good example of this exists at St Mary's. The heavy, somewhat clumsy, chancel roof of 1846 caused the chancel to need underpinning to stop it sinking, whereas the medieval nave roof is lighter, stronger and only puts the correct amount of stress on the nave walls. The font looks old but is now thought to be quite late, the ancient font may now be in Elsted church, as the font there matches an early description of the one at Stoughton. There are some old ledger slabs in very good condition, a few interesting memorials in the chancel and a large painting of the Last Supper in the north chapel. The brick-built porch is seventeenth century and perhaps looks a little out of place. For some unfathomable reason the churchyard was levelled in 1954 and the stones made into a kind of 'crazy paving' around the porch.

WEST STOKE *St Andrew* ❀❀❀ ⊕⊕⊕ 📖 (WSSA)119

Much of the nave is from the eleventh century Saxon church and the tall relatively thin walls and steep roof are typical Saxon work. The north door which now leads from the church into the vestry is from the same period although the mid-thirteenth century carved head of an unknown bishop above it has been re-sited from elsewhere in the church. The south doorway is thirteenth century and the door itself may be of the same date. Note the original hinges and that the door is peppered with buckshot, the reason for the latter is a complete mystery.

The porch is very interesting, it is of two storeys and is in reality a small tower complete with bell dated 1712. Although this one was built in the thirteenth century this is exactly the way the first Saxon church towers developed. The forerunner of the porch, a chapel known as a porticus often had a second storey added forming a short tower just like this one. The chancel was also rebuilt in the thirteenth century and a priest's door (now blocked) was added 100 years later. Apart from the remains of a small Saxon window in the east wall all the windows are thirteenth century, although those in the north and south walls were modified in the nineteenth century. The chancel arch was rebuilt and the font, pews and pulpit added during this Victorian refurbishment. There are few memorials in the church but the wall tomb on the north wall of the chancel makes up in quality what is lacking in quantity. The brightly coloured memorial to Adrian Stoughton and his wife was erected in 1635 and shows their sixteen children below them. In a style typical of the time, but a little gruesome to us, those children who died before their parents are portrayed as skulls carried by their brothers and sisters. Also in the chancel is a fine trefoil-headed piscina. Outside, the church is surrounded by old gravestones and there is a scratch dial to be found on the east side of the porch doorway. There is one military marker, for an airman dated 1946. The churchyard is quite small, well kept and sparsely populated and the picture as a whole is well-balanced and a joy to the eye.

DIDLING *St Andrew* ❀❀ ⌖ 📖📖 (WSSA)79

The church is situated in a remote corner of the county on the edge of the Downs. There is no village nearby and it stands with just a single farm for a companion.

Built in the thirteenth century as a two-cell church a new south wall in the fourteenth century has all but converted the church into a single cell. The north wall retains its original lancets while the south wall has its fourteenth century versions plus from the sixteenth century one window and the doorway. The east and west windows were re-set in their respective walls when they were re-built in brick in the eighteenth century. The interior fittings are the main feature of the church. The medieval pews are rough made, very plain and perhaps the oldest I've ever seen. The altar rail is Jacobean and the pulpit, in Jacobean style, was made from a seventeenth century parish chest. The font is roughly made to the point of being misshapen and must be very old. The church is lit with Victorian oil lamps although electric power is perhaps soon to come. The churchyard has some interesting grave markers, an ancient coffin slab is laid flat to the southeast and there is a small group of iron markers to the east. Close to these is a stone dated 1703, very early for a gravestone.

TROTTON *St George* ❀❀ ✠ 📖📖📖 (WSSA)57

St George's may be one of the most interesting in the county to the church enthusiast, thanks to its contents. Of the structure, the tower built in 1230 is the oldest part of the building but there is a hint of an older structure in the first few courses. The bulk of the church was rebuilt in about 1300, probably at the expense of the Camoys family. Sir Ralph Camoys married Margaret De Braose about this time and it is she who is thought to have been instrumental in the rebuilding. She died in 1310 and one of the church's great treasures is a brass in her memory. This can be found under a large red carpet in the central aisle. As is usual with very early brasses it is full size and very detailed, look for her small dog in the dress folds and the two hairpins holding her hair in place. This brass is almost certainly the oldest brass depicting a female in the country. In direct contrast to Margaret's hidden brass is the one for Thomas, Lord Camoys and his wife Elizabeth. This is set into a massive Purbeck marble tomb directly in front of the altar. Dating from 1420 this almost complete canopied brass of the couple is rated as one of the best in the land and shows them hand in hand rather than in prayer as is usual. Thomas, who commanded the left flank of the victorious English army at the battle of Agincourt is in full armour. A small boy can be seen in the folds of Elizabeth's gown. This boy is thought to be their illegitimate son Roger, the last Lord Camoys. Elizabeth was the great-granddaughter of Edward III and widow of Henry Percy (known as Hotspur). This would make her the inspiration for Shakespeare's character Kate in Henry IV. As if these treasures are not enough the whole of the nave is covered with wall paintings executed about 1390 by virtue of a bequest of thirty sheep from yet another female member of the Camoys family. These are in quite good repair especially those on the west wall, these depict the Last Judgement, the seven deadly sins and the seven great virtues. Truly a picture lesson in how to behave and what would happen if you did not. There is a good example of a low sided window in the north wall still retaining its wooden shutter. The churchyard contains many very old stones, some with the gruesome skull and bones motifs common on early eighteenth century grave markers.

COCKING ✠✠ 📖 (WSSA)80

Built in the late eleventh century to replace a Saxon church on the same spot much of the nave, the chancel arch and parts of the chancel remain from the early Norman church. The lower parts of the nave walls were lost when first the south aisle was inserted in about 1300, using the then new Decorated architectural style, and in 1865 when the present Victorian north aisle was added. During the south aisle enlargement the Lady Chapel and tower of local malmstone were built and new chancel windows were put in. The blocked Norman slit windows can still be seen in the chancel walls. One original Norman window can be seen high on the south wall of the nave. One splay of this window contains a very interesting wall painting that once must have been part of a nativity series. Wall paintings are often difficult to date but this one can be fixed quite accurately at around 1220, as the painting was not new when the window was blocked up during the 1300 building work and not uncovered until 1896. The font is thought by some to be Saxon but is more likely very early Norman and sits on a later base. The piscina, uncovered and restored during the careful restoration of the chancel in 1896, is of the same thirteenth century date as the one in the south aisle. The Easter sepulchre in the north wall is perhaps the oldest in Sussex. There are several interesting grave slabs now mounted on the walls, all seem to be for former rectors mostly of the eighteenth century. In the north wall of the sanctuary is a pre-conquest coffin lid with an early Christian Y-shaped cross carved into it. The church dedication has been lost over the centuries but no doubt it will come to light in the future as so many others have as researchers dig through the mountains of medieval church records archived around the county.

BEPTON *St Mary* ❀ ✝✝ 📖 (WSSA)80

The Norman church at Bepton was started in 1182 to replace the wooden Saxon church on the site. The usual tests must have been carried out to see if the ground could support the usual metre thick Norman walls but it soon became clear that the chalk could not bear the weight of the proposed tower. Building was slow in the twelfth century usually taking several 'seasons' to complete. This gave the builders time to see just how last year's building work was settling in and the tower was way out of line before the church was even finished. The tower was capped off at little more than one storey high but in 1250, with no more subsidence evident, the second storey was added but with much thinner walls. The brick buttresses supporting the tower today were added in 1620, possibly to make sure the tower could stand the weight of a second bell which was installed in 1632.The other bell is dated 1589. Of the nave and chancel only a small area of the old walls survived the re-build of 1890s, although the original roof beams in the chancel were uncovered. One chancel window and the Easter sepulchre tomb were also retained during the refurbishment. The sepulchre is particularly interesting with its large canopy carved in the shape of flames. It bears an inscription in Norman French which translates to 'here lies Rado de la Hedol, God grant him mercy'. Rado may well have been the lord of the manor immediately following the Conquest in 1066. His 2-metre grave slab is mounted on the wall nearby and the sepulchre looks to have been added to his tomb in the thirteenth century. The very simple and worn font is the oldest thing in the church and almost certainly comes from the Saxon church. In the porch is an interesting notice dated 1878 which proclaims that £10 was allocated for the refurbishment of the seating all of which was to be free by law. The churchyard is sparsely populated with markers partly because of Puritan vandalism and partly due to the local stone wearing out quickly. A mass grave used at the time of the Black Death in the 1340s was found under the bushes on the left as you approach the south porch.

THE CHURCHYARD AS A BURIAL PLACE

In the early days of Christianity the churchyard was not primarily a burial place. At that time it was an extension of the church, perhaps the place where the travelling priest first preached to the curious locals before the first building was even built (Ford), or even the site of pre-Christian pagan rites (North Stoke). After the church became established it became a less formal meeting area than the church itself, more of a village focal point. Fairs were held in churchyards as were early village council meetings, even trials were held there. At Rye church in East Sussex a murder victim lies next to his murderer close to the spot where the trial was held. Armies were mustered in churchyards and archery practice (compulsory by law in medieval times) was a common pastime in churchyards after services. The marks left from sharpening arrows can clearly be seen on the walls at Berwick and Edburton. As late as 1610 King James I, in his book on sports, encourages the playing of certain sports after church in the churchyard; these sports included fist fights and cockfighting. Several cockfighting pits still exist in churchyards in other parts of the country. The rector grazed his animals in the churchyard; these were often bequests from parishioners and an important source of income. Shipley church still has a permanent flock of sheep with a redundant porch as a shelter. Churchyards were not originally fenced in and it would seem the church law ordering the enclosing of all churchyards in the fourteenth century had much to do with keeping the right animals in and the wrong ones out. Accounts exist of burials being unearthed by wild animals much to the distress of the priest and villagers. The tapsel gate, a type of portal unique to Sussex churchyards, is clearly more practical when dealing with animals than humans. The boundary wall or fence was often maintained by the congregation. At Cowfold the wooden fence still carries the names of the farms responsible for each section.

This does not mean that burials did not take place in the churchyard, they did, and from its earliest times. It is most likely that the new Christian believers wanted their dead buried as close to their religious site as possible as they had done in pagan times. The church was happy to oblige. This was after all the practice elsewhere in the Christian world, a practice that had developed for exactly the same pagan reasons. At first only the rich or influential had any grave marker at all, usually the stone lid of the actual coffin protruding from the floor inside the church (examples at Poynings still survive in situ). Soon a few of these started to appear outside the church as close to the south or east wall as possible (Chithurst*). The ordinary folk were buried in unmarked plots in the churchyard on the south side with only the tall churchyard cross as a marker for all. Most of the tall church crosses in Sussex were probably made of wood and have not survived but fragments of the earliest stone Sussex cross of all, set up by St Wilfrid in Selsey (chapel), can be seen re-used in the churchyard war memorial at Selsey (town). The north side of the churchyard was considered the dark side and was reserved for suicides and serious criminals until quite modern times. The grave of a smuggler can still be seen today on the north side of Patcham church (East Sussex) inscribed 'unfortunately shot'. Coffins were rare and the remains of the dead soon returned to the earth, the ground to be re-used time and again. Even a small village church has probably seen four or five thousand burials in eight hundred years. The raised ground that often surrounds a church is usually caused by the displaced earth of centuries.

By the late sixteenth century coffins were more in evidence, leading to separate plots. The ordinary people, although themselves mostly illiterate, were aware of the importance of the written word and wanted some sort of individual marker for their departed loved ones. At first this took the form of a wooden marker, this was especially true in Sussex where stone is hard to come by. By the late seventeenth century the simple wooden cross had developed into posts at the head and foot end of the grave with a board fixed between bearing the name, date and inscription. These were traditionally called 'leaping boards', a hint perhaps of those sporting events held in the churchyards of old. These wooden markers did of course not stand the test of time and most are long gone, but Sussex has more than its share of survivors notably at Twineham, Slaugham and Cuckfield ,where a perfectly restored example shows how they must have looked when new. By 1700 the first stone markers were appearing in the same shape as the former wooden ones but with the bar usually at ground level and forming a flat narrow coffin lid shape (Bolney). The next development was for the post at the head end to become a short flat stone bearing the inscriptions much like today's gravestones; at the foot end there was a smaller version and the central bar is often absent altogether. By 1750 the footstone had mostly disappeared and we are left with two basic styles, a very short heavy stone with only the date and the deceased's initials (very like the last of the footstones), and the taller richly carved traditional gravestones that mark the high point of gravestone design. Sussex is particularly well furnished with these fascinating stones, often carved with what we today would call grotesque scenes. Skulls and skeletons are common place, scythes and gravediggers' tools abound. At Westbourne, a churchyard that contains every kind of gravestone and tomb, one stone shows an open coffin with body inside. One of the most gruesome in this morbid style is at Ardingly where death is portrayed as a skeleton stabbing a woman with a lance while angels look on. Sometimes the deceased's profession is also often portrayed, a farmer at Westbourne, a carpenter at Lewes, (St John), a sea captain at Bosham, a drowned sailor at West Wittering. At Warbleton a tree falling on a man shows the cause of death. For every skull portrayed a cherub can be found to even the score, together with trumpets, hourglasses and angels. The only religious symbol noticeable by its absence is the cross, considered too 'popish' for the Protestants of the 1700s. The message carved into these stones is clear, time is short, live a good life or else. These eighteenth century stones, now worn and covered in moss, add to the tranquillity of the churchyard today, but it should be remembered that when new they were often brightly painted. Many priests deplored this practice, as within a few months the paint would begin to flake off and fade leaving a very sorry sight. Cheap alternatives to natural stone were markers made of Coade stone, this kiln-fired brick looks very much like real stone and was produced between 1750 and 1850. It did not weather well and few survive; examples can be found at Old Shoreham, Ifield and the memorial to Sarah Goring(d1798) inside Wiston church.

By this time only the very rich or well-connected were being buried inside the church, and in the churchyard the well-to-do were being buried in chest tombs to show their greater stature. Good examples can be seen at Westbourne and Itchingfield. On rare occasions land in the churchyard was purchased by a rich family as the site of a family vault, to hold several generations of the same family, a fine example is the Prime family vault at Walberton. In Victorian times, urban cemeteries were opening up and churchyard burials declined. The large memorials of the late nineteenth century seem to have more to do with outdoing your neighbour than marking a grave and few of these late markers are of much interest. Exceptions are the cast-iron markers made as cheap alternatives to stone in the late Victorian era, these cost as little as ten shillings (50p). They have lasted well, although few are readable, at Wisborough Green there are thirteen and at the small church at Cocking no less than twenty.

Some churches are surrounded by stones; others have but a few. Some had stones vandalised during the Civil War, others inexplicably had all their stones removed as late as the

1950s. Exploration of the inside of the boundary wall will often uncover rows and rows of beautiful carved stones, sometimes roughly stacked in piles. The church rubbish tip will usually have several broken stones embedded in it. Many have been used to make paths, with varying success, the best is at East Lavant.
In recent years interest in the history contained in our churchyards has increased. For the first time maps of the graves, listing as many inscriptions, dates and names as possible, are being made before they become un-readable, important stones are being cleaned and restored. It has also been noted that because of their untouched nature certain wild flowers, and the insects that feed on them, now only exist in churchyards and areas are being set aside as nature reserves (Bolney) as part of a nationwide plan. We can only hope that modern views on preserving our past will mean that the village churchyard, a history book of the area, will remain untouched for all to see in centuries to come.

* the stones at Chithurst may not be in their original positions.

WEST OF THE ARUN

West of the river Arun stretch a long line of churches from Climping near the coast to Singleton in the north. In the south are Yapton in its village setting, and isolated Ford, two of the most picturesque churches in the county. In the middle are Eastergate and Walberton with their farmland backgrounds. In the downland to the north are ancient East Dean, Upwaltham and Saxon centrepiece Singleton.

SINGLETON *The Blessed Virgin Mary* ❀ ✠✠✠ 📖📖 (WSSA)100

In Saxon times Singleton church was the main church of the hundred of Singleton, an area owned by Earl Godwin, the most important statesman in England and father of King Harold,the last Saxon king. The pointed Saxon doorway to be seen from the nave high in the tower wall led to a long room above the nave that housed priests that served other churches in the surrounding area. A small window above the chancel arch lit this room and still contains some medieval glass. Another major Saxon church at nearby Bosham has an identical doorway that served the same purpose. The tower itself was added to the nave about 1000. The high Saxon walls of the nave, built with stone brought from Quarr in the Isle of Wight, survive but were pierced in the thirteenth century to give access to the aisles built at that time. The two light windows in the aisles replaced smaller openings in the fourteenth century. The fifteenth century rood staircase near the chancel arch remains completely intact and is one of the best examples I've yet seen. Most of the pews are at least in part early Tudor, some with carved ends. The early nineteenth century west gallery replaced a much earlier one that was in disrepair. There are three Elizabethan tombs, one in the north aisle, one in the south and one in the tower, and in the sanctuary two tombs for Earls of Arundel, Thomas (d 1524) and William (d 1544). These are quite badly damaged and seem to have been moved to the church from the Fitzalan hunting lodge chapel that stood nearby. The tomb of Thomas Johnson (d1744) is interesting, the inscription makes it quite clear he was a keen huntsman. There is a great deal of medieval graffiti in the church, as well as the usual crosses and pilgrim marks, the meaning of which has been lost over the centuries. There is a rare ragged staff of Warwick and a Solomon's knot on the north porch door jamb and a vow cross on the south-east semi-pillar in the nave. The Rev Sicklemore, who became a staunch backer of Oliver Cromwell during the Civil War, scratched his name on the chancel arch. Much of the roof is fourteenth century, as is one of the two bells in the tower. Outside there are a great number of very old gravestones, some with interesting inscriptions but unfortunately they have all been moved into an untidy line at the back of the churchyard.

EAST DEAN *All Saints* ❀❀ ✠ 📖📖 (WSSA)101

The cruciform-shaped church sits on high ground above the quiet village of East Dean. The village is of Saxon origin, the land owned by King Alfred and there must have been a church here in Saxon times but nothing remains of it today. The oldest surviving parts are the Norman tower and both transepts, although the latter were re-furbished in the fourteenth century. The church's best feature is the south doorway; built about 1200 and protected by a later porch it has some fine roll mouldings and carvings. From the thirteenth century both chancel side walls and the west and north nave walls survive. The blocked arches from a former north aisle can clearly be seen from outside the building. The font is of uncertain age, dated 1660 it may be a re-make of an older Norman font. The plinth is certainly old and looks to be an upturned pillar capital perhaps from nearby Boxgrove priory. Much of the floor is paved with old gravestones from the churchyard, some of which are very worn. In the north transept is an oak cupboard from the time of Charles II and in the south transept the ancient bell clappers and mounts from the bell tower are displayed. The churchyard drops down the hill to an untended area left for nature conservation. Close to the church are a large number of interesting old stones, many with skulls, gravedigger's tools and bones carved into them. Under the yew is one with an hourglass on it to remind us our time is short. Set into the church wall is the gravestone of William Peachey, a famous blacksmith who made swords for some of Cromwell's officers during the Civil War.

EARTHAM *St Margaret* ❀ ⌖ 📖📖📖 (WSSA)122

Although greatly restored in 1869 a fair amount of the original Norman church remains. Most of the nave is twelfth century including the main door in the west wall. This favoured entry position in Norman times is rarely seen in small churches today, most have been moved to the south or north walls. This door is not the normal arched door in an arched frame. The frame is arched but the top part is squared off to form a tympanum filled with faced stone, the large mortared joints are signs of its great age. At the other end of the nave another feature of the old church is the chancel arch. What from a distance seems to be two arches is in fact a single structure, this is called a double order arch and this one is a little unusual. The two half-rounded pillars seem to be an early attempt to copy a classical design, note the ornate capitals and the carvings of a hare on one and an old man on the other. In the thirteenth century the south aisle was added, and is rather nicely proportioned; two wide arches spring from a large central pillar and attach to the nave via half pillars at each end. The central pillar contains some very old graffiti and a little of the original red wall colour of the aisle can still be seen at the top. On the floor of the chancel is the coat of arms of Queen Victoria in tile form, which makes a nice change from the usual hanging boards. St Margaret's has more than its share of interesting monuments. A large memorial to Thomas Hayley, the artist son of the poet William Hayley, is by the famous sculptor John Flaxman. Thomas was Flaxman's pupil and the inscription mentions this. There are many memorials to the Milbanke family including Peniston Milbanke whose son, Jack, was Winston Churchill's best friend at school. The most interesting memorial is the one in the chancel to William Huskisson. Huskisson was a famous politician and financial adviser to the government but will be best remembered for being the world's first victim of a railway accident. While attending the opening of the Liverpool and Manchester railway on the 15th Sept 1830 he was hit by Stephenson's famous 'Rocket' steam engine and died a few hours later.

UPWALTHAM *St Mary the Virgin* ❀❀ ✠✠✠ 📖 (WSSA)102

Take away the bellcote and the fifteenth century south door, block a couple of windows and replace the roof with thatch and St Mary's would look exactly as it did when it was built over 800 years ago. One of only five churches in Sussex to retain its apse, the church has no chancel, the apse being large enough to do the job. This seems to be the reason why all the five Sussex apses have survived. The church was built in 1200 at a time when the purpose of the apse was changing, for a while it retained its shape but became larger and developed into the chancel as we know it today. With the decrease of secrecy and mysticism associated with the small apse-shaped recess which appeared in the first Christian churches in Rome these small niche-like appendages were serving no purpose by the late twelfth century and were being removed. They were replaced by a room large enough for the clerics to carry out their duties whilst still retaining a separation from the congregation (chancels were screened off from the nave for the next 350 years, at first totally).

The lancets in the apse are Early English as is the low sided window, the sill of which was shaped to form a seat for the priest, this was squared off in the nineteenth century. The three-light north window is sixteenth century and the west Victorian. There is a very unusual piscina hollowed out of the capital of an ancient pillar, perhaps from the original chancel arch, which was replaced around 1300. The church walls are typically Norman being almost a metre thick. Three tie beams in the nave and one in the apse, each with a king post, hold the roof. The ceiling is of a shape called 'mansard' and there is a full set of chandeliers. The font is as old as the church, as are the corbels that held the rood beam across the chancel arch. Every tree in the churchyard was lost in the 1987 hurricane and their replacements have been provided by twenty-one local families. There are seventy-one stones in the churchyard dating from 1700 to the present day.

EASTERGATE *St George* ❀❀ ✠✠ 📖 (WSSA)142

Many churches are close to farms but this one literally sits in a farmyard. The nearby farmhouse is sixteenth century and there is an interesting two storey medieval granary nearby, perched precariously on mushroom-shaped saddlestones. The south wall of the chancel is worthy of note, being built in the Norman 'herringbone' style mostly of flints but partly of re-used Roman bricks. The chancel at least must date from the twelfth century and retains one Norman slit window on the north side. Windows are the main features here with several styles on show. The nave windows are refurbished fourteenth century lancets, one with a fragment of original stained glass in the shape of the arms of the Fitzalan and de Warenne families. The east window was added one hundred years later and the west was paid for with money left for the purpose in 1534. The bellcote is a nineteenth century replacement and is a rather nice example, far better than the open stone bell housings added by the Victorians to many of the other churches in the area. The churchyard is very well looked after and contains stones from the eighteenth century to the present day. Although not as remote as some other Sussex churches this is truly a country setting with farmyard sounds and smells in the background, well worth a visit.

SLINDON *St Mary* ❀ ✠ 📖📖 (WSSA)123

This church has links with St Anselm (to whom the building of the church is attributed) and the influential Archbishop Stephen Langton (who died nearby in 1228). It was another Archbishop, Theobold, who in 1154 knocked down the old church mentioned in the Domesday Book and built the church that at least in part survives today. From that building one small window above the north aisle and parts of the nave walls remain. In the twelfth century arches were cut through the nave walls to accommodate a one-bay chapel to the north and a two-bay aisle to the south. Two hundred years later two more arches were added to the north aisle to make the chapel into a full aisle and one to the south to even things up all round. Note the different architectural styles used in the arches. A small wooden-topped tower was also added during these fourteenth century changes. Extensive restoration in 1866 replaced the wooden part of the tower with stone. Most of the present windows date from this Victorian rebuild, as do the aisle walls and the north entrance, but the door itself is medieval. There are four bells in the tower, three of these are seventeenth century and the two dated 1651 and 1657 are rare as they were cast during the time of Cromwell's commonwealth when bell casting was restricted by law. The royal coat of arms is that of George III and at the west end of the south aisle there are a few fourteenth century poppy-headed benches. By far the church's rarest possession is the wooden effigy of Anthony St Leger (d1539). He lies full length in armour from the time of the War of the Roses, his head resting on his helmet. This wooden version of the more commonly seen stone effigies is unique in Sussex and has now been moved from its place in the chancel to a position where it can be better protected.

WALBERTON *St Mary* ❀ ⌖ 📖 (WSSA)143

The village of Walberton is three miles downstream from Arundel, and the church was important enough in Norman times to be listed in the Domesday Book as having a permanent priest. Considerable Saxon stonework survived until 1903 when a major rebuild destroyed all but the slightest hints of any pre-Conquest work. The west wall was once described as being made mostly of re-used Roman stones, but today the only part that might be Saxon would be where the now blocked west doorway shows through. The north and south aisles must have been added over a considerable period of time in the thirteenth century for each column and arch, although Norman, are of different styles and ages. The chancel with its original lancet windows is also thirteenth century as is the very rare north porch. The font is a crudely made affair and is almost certainly Saxon. What were at first thought to be simple decorations to its sides are now believed to be just deep cuts from the mason's axe. Chisels which allowed more detailed work were not used until the late eleventh century. There is a large stone coffin on show found close to the church during Victorian drainage work. The large churchyard could well be used to catalogue the development of grave markers containing as it does examples of stones from the earliest stones of the eighteenth century up to the present day. There is a particularly nice row of head and foot markers all with central stone bar to the right of the main path to the church. Close to the east end of the church dozens of the typical short early stones, many bearing only dates and initials, have been repositioned to form a path edge round the chancel. On the north side is the magnificent marble vault of the Prime family with its heavy low iron door. There is also an interesting modern lych gate.

YAPTON *St Mary* ❀❀❀ ✠✠✠ 📖 (WSSA)165

Most of the nave and the short tower with its tall pointed Sussex cap are late twelfth century and built in the Transitional style (1170-1220). This architectural style had moved on from the heavy round-arched Norman period but had yet to fully develop into the lighter sharply pointed arch and tall lancet window style of the Early English period which was in full fashion by 1230 and dominates so many Sussex churches. The tower, which has developed a pronounced lean to the south and is heavily buttressed, retains its original Norman slit window on the ground floor, and two fine round-headed Norman bell openings split into two lights by central baluster shafts. The wood-framed west porch is fourteenth century and is one of the church's best features. The roof slopes very close to the ground, especially on the south side, which may indicate that it was thatched in medieval times. Large low level dormer windows were inserted into the roof span in the seventeenth century to increase the light in the nave. Two original round windows close to the ground can be seen in the south wall. Inside the church the nave is quite plain with a narrow south aisle separated from the nave by good examples of Transitional arches, not quite round-headed but not sharply pointed either. The great interior treasure is the early Norman font. Tub-shaped and straight-sided it is decorated with eight cartouches containing crosses in the form of swords. Around the rim is a wide chevron design typical of the Norman period. There are few memorials of note the best is perhaps the 1687 wall plaque in memory of John Edmonds. The chancel was rebuilt in the thirteenth century in truly Early English style and still has at least some of its lancet windows, the east window is a nineteenth century replacement. The churchyard is particularly nice, well cared for and divided up with trees and large bushes. There are some old stones including one good eighteenth century example to the left of the porch. Few churches are as photogenic as St Mary's, especially when viewed from the west.

FORD *St Andrew* ❀❀ ✠✠ 📖📖 (WSSA)144

This tiny candlelit two-cell church sits in a bleak isolation on the coastal plain a mile or so from the sea near the river Arun. There is strong evidence of an early Saxon stone cross on the site and a piece of this cross can be seen close to the fifteenth century north doorway inside the church. This cross may have marked a meeting place or field church which pre-dated any purpose-built church. Small areas of the stone Saxon church that followed can still be seen in the nave which was rebuilt in 1100.The chancel was added about one hundred years later and extended further east in 1320 when the east window was added. The chancel arch is Norman and has a star decoration, one of the more uncommon designs. Two small Saxon windows survive in the north wall and the font is pre-Conquest. The later was discarded centuries ago and only came to light in 1899 when it was found in a farmyard. The two painted consecration crosses used during the blessing of the church are very rare and may well be from the 1100 re-build. Following a fire the south aisle was rebuilt about 1550 and a series of wall paintings were added at the same time. The north-east window of the nave is particularly interesting, it has been cut down to floor level to accommodate a small staircase which led up to the top of the rood screen in medieval times. This technique was only used in very small churches where funds and space were short. There are several different styles of cross scratched into the south door jamb, probably pilgrim graffiti, and on the outside south-east corner of the nave there is a group of scratch sun dials. The bell turret is painted white as a navigational aid to shipping, as it has been since it was built. It contains two bells, one seventeenth century; the other is one of the oldest bells in the county and was cast about 1350. The churchyard is tiny and contains only a few stones, which has the effect of making the church look even lonelier. This church, often overlooked in guidebooks, contains a great deal of interest and should be high on any list of churches to visit in the area.

CLIMPING *St Mary* ❀❀ ✠✠✠ 📖📖 (WSSA)166

The picturesque village of Climping sits close to the sea a little to the east of Littlehampton and its thirteenth century church is a must for the serious church visitor. The church is cruciform in shape and is almost entirely unchanged since its building in 1220. Hill's nineteenth century restoration was mercifully (and for him unusually) slight and is of little consequence. The south porch opens directly into the south aisle, the arcade of which is more ornately decorated than is usual for an Early English style church. There are more than twenty lancet windows all in their original positions and clearly showing what a large church of the period looked like when first built. The three closely grouped lancets that make up the east window are particularly good and have nook shafts to further adorn them. There is a good piscina with matching aumbry and the font is contemporary with the main body of the church. The church possesses some interesting woodwork, a panel in the north transept dated 1634 is probably from a private box pew and there are some fifteenth century bench ends in the nave. By far the best piece of woodwork is the thirteenth century chest; this large chest, often wrongly called a crusader's chest, is beautifully carved and is considered the best example in the country. Due to its high value it has now been removed to the safer confines of Chichester Cathedral where it is on show. Another almost unique item and impossible to move is the fifteenth century stone pulpit, one of only two in Sussex. Perched at the end of the short south transept is the tower. Certainly the building's best overall feature it stands on a different alignment to rest of the building as if a separate entity. Unusually for a tower it out dates the church by forty years at least in its lower two thirds. The tower west door is a masterpiece of Norman stonework with its shaped inner arch and sharp cut zigzag decoration on the outer round arch. Above it is a narrow window almost obscured by more zigzags. The newel-style staircase, so often a later addition, was built with the tower and all in all the tower represents a major architectural achievement for 1180. The churchyard is a very pleasant and peaceful place especially in the late summer when its flowering bushes are at their best. There are a lot of eighteenth century stones, many very clearly cut and easy to read.

ARUN VALLEY

The river Arun cuts its way through the middle of the South Downs passing some of the oldest surviving Sussex churches at Bury and Hardham. At Amberley both castle and church look out over the river as they have since Norman times. In the west there are remote but not-to-be missed Coates and Barlavington and in the east the ancient village of West Chiltington. Perhaps the churches with the best feeling of timelessness are the tiny candlelit churches of Wiggonholt and Greatham, built for the shepherds of the marshlands around the river.

BARLAVINGTON *St Mary* ❀❀❀ ✠✠ 📖 (WSSA)103

This simple two-cell church was built about 1200 when the total population of England was little more than one million. If you have ever wondered just how quiet the world was in those days then take a trip to Barlavington. With just a couple of cottages and the barns of a farm for company the church stands in an almost totally silent landscape. Aisles to both north and south sides of the nave were added in the Early English style but the north was removed some time later, its arches still visible from outside. The south aisle was re-built in 1874 but the columns at least are thirteenth century. The proportions of the wide chancel seem just right and its two wide spaced lancets suit it well. There is a beautiful modern carving of the Annunciation on the east wall, which sets the whole thing off nicely. The south door appears to be very old and its hinges ancient. The west window is interesting, as it is one of those that seem to be a transitional design between the Early English lancets and the fine tracery of the Decorated period that followed. Here the two lancets are close together with a small circular window above, all three enclosed in a thick frame that was soon to become the delicate shape of the well-known Gothic windows of the fourteenth century. The church bell housed in a bellcote at the west of the church is clearly visible from the churchyard. In 1724 there were two bells; one was found to be cracked and was removed, the survivor is inscribed in Latin 'Bryan Eldridge made me 1651'. The Eldridge family made bells in Wokingham between 1615 and about 1710. There are some old stones in the churchyard, which has a fine view of the Downs. For peace and simplicity St Mary's must rate very highly.

SUTTON *St John the Baptist* ❀ ✠✠ 📖 (WSSA)103

This surprisingly large church stands at the centre of the parish and is a good example of a church that has changed with the centuries. The oldest surviving part is the late eleventh century exterior of the nave north wall with its typical herringbone masonry. Most of the other nave walls date from the twelfth century. The tower with its original arch, the chancel and north transept are all fourteenth century with the tower being about fifty years older than the other two. The tower screen is interesting as it is made up from parts of the much older chancel screen. There is one bell, which was recast in 1712. The south aisle although looking very much like its surroundings is a Victorian re-build. The nave roof is also a replacement although the tie beams are probably original. In the chancel the 'wagon' style roof is fourteenth century and there is evidence that it was at least partly gilded at some time. A drawing from the 1880s shows the rood beam in place but now only the massive corbels that supported it remain. The ancient font is thirteenth century and stands next to a huge column that pre-dates it by over a century. The church has few memorials inside the church but as usual there is always something of interest to be found. Close inspection of the war memorial shows two members of the same family W.Heather and R.Heather who died just one day apart in 1914, yet they served in different regiments. What a tragedy that must have been for the village at the time. The churchyard has some interesting grave markers including two iron markers more common in East Sussex and a military marker for a member of the RAF killed in World War II. Perhaps the most interesting grave marker is a very rare wooden one with a lead plate attached bearing the deceased's details. The date on this is 1919 so it has done well to survive. The low arch in the external chancel wall once housed an eighteenth century tomb, and is much further east than was usually allowed and was probably the tomb of a cleric of some standing. The yew trees, planted in 1666 by Joseph Sefton, are mere youngsters compared to the 3000-year-old yew at nearby Coldwaltham.

COATES *St Agatha* ❀❀ ✠✠ (WSSA)84

The hamlet of Coates is tiny and secluded and its church matches, for it too is tiny and secluded. It was built in the late twelfth century and had its only major refurbishment just one hundred years later. Since then little has changed, a new bellcote was added in 1907 containing just one bell instead of the two listed there in 1725 and a vestry has been tacked on, probably in the nineteenth century. Although the thick Norman walls must once have been plastered they look particularly nice now with their not quite herringbone style of stonework. One original window survives in the south wall but all the others were part of the thirteenth century changes. I find that these Early English style lancet windows always seem to make the best east windows. Whether it is tall singles, stepped triples or as here at St Agatha's the less common spaced doubles they have an imposing simple grandeur that suits the sanctuary end of the church. The chancel arch is Norman and large for so small a church. The font too is probably as old as the church; it is square and fixed to the wall on one side. The stone priest's seat in the chancel is an unusual single-seat sedile rather than the usual three seat sedilia. The sedile, holy water stoop and priest's door are also thirteenth century additions. The queen post roof is old and has six tie beams. The north doorway was enlarged in the late fifteenth century and appears still to have its five hundred-year-old wooden door. The north doorway has probably always been the main entrance and may have been put on the unfashionable north side because it faced the village, whereas the more usual south door would not have. This practical idea is not uncommon, for example at Clayton the door changed sides when the road moved from one side of the church to the other. The churchyard at Coates is well cared for and as one might expect in such a secluded spot sparsely populated.

FITTLEWORTH *St Mary* ✠ 📖📖 (WSSA)84

A painting in the nave dated 1870 shows the early English chancel and the twelfth century tower with nothing in between. Removal of the galleries that went almost all round the old nave probably showed defects in the structure that led to demolition of the old nave and the building of the present one in 1871. The ancient tower stands as solid as ever with its peal of six bells, the oldest of which dates from about 1350. Inside there is a stone recess believed to be a seat for the ringers, a rare luxury in the fourteenth century. The clock on the west face was installed in 1897 to mark the diamond jubilee of Queen Victoria. The chancel with its typical Early English lancet windows, (the western-most lancet is of the 'low sided' type often wrongly called 'leper' windows) still boasts a piscina and near it is a small brass dated 1628. The nineteenth century nave has little to offer but does retain the sixteenth century north porch, which has some very old woodwork and contains a massive stone coffin lid which may be over nine hundred years old. This probably started life protruding from the chancel dirt floor and may have seen use hundreds of years later as a 'resurrection' stone placed on new graves for a period to stop grave robbers stealing the corpse. Inside the church the font sits between the north and south porches and on the wall of the new vestry is a very old cross, possibly Saxon work. There are two chests, one dated 1615 and the other was previously owned by C.E.Kempe, the famous artist whose firm made stained glass windows for churches all over Sussex including three here at Fittleworth. These can be identified by the wheatsheaf mark in the corner of the window. Also of interest are the royal arms of George III (considered one of the best in the county), and a small plaque by the south door presented by the London school whose children were evacuated to Fittleworth during World War II. There are some nice eighteenth and nineteenth century stones in the churchyard but the giant yew tree pre-dates everything at over 1000 years old and was almost certainly a place of pre-Christian worship and the reason the church was built on this spot in the first place.

STOPHAM *St Mary the Virgin* ❀ ⌖ 🕮🕮 (WSSA)85

Stopham must have been a very important village right from Saxon times and boasts a very rare seven-span bridge across the Arun built in 1309, which along with the church is well worth a visit. The oldest parts of the church are eleventh century and although probably Norman there is more than a hint of Saxon style in the tall walls. The tower and much of the eastern end of the building were rebuilt in the seventeenth century but almost certainly in the original style. It was perhaps during this rebuild that all traces of the anchorite's cell mentioned in an early will were lost. Towers built in the 1600s are quite rare and this one has a few architectural features worthy of note, namely the wooden belfry shutters and a now bricked-in door in an unusual position. The original peal of three bells is now reduced to one bell in working order, dated 1614. Both of the tall north and south church doorways appear to be original and contain interesting Norman work. All of the windows have been changed over the years but traces of the old lancets can still be made out in places. The churchyard has more interesting memorials than most, as does the interior of the church where the Barttelot family prevails. There are twelve brasses and many more stone memorials to this family. One of these dated 1707 has an interesting spelling of Walter Barttelot's wife's name, 'Jsabely'. The regimental colours on show were laid up in 1985 and are those of the 1st Battalion Coldstream guards. The large well-proportioned octagonal font is thirteenth century and has nice deep cut decorative work around the bowl. In 1982 new hassocks were produced in a profusion of designs and these add a bright touch to the church.

BURY *St John the Evangelist* ❀❀❀ ✟ 📖 (WSSA)105

This fine looking church stands on high ground just a few metres from the ancient Bury Wharf, site of the important ferry crossing that bridged the Arun for centuries and was still in service as late as 1955. Most of the nave and the tower arch were built about 1200 but the sturdy tower itself is perhaps 50 years older. Soon after the nave was built the south wall was removed so that it could be widened by means of an aisle. The short architectural period during which the aisle was built links the Norman and Early English styles and is called the Transitional period and spans the years 1170 to 1220. Norman building techniques called for thick wide pillars although the pointed arches above them hint at the later Early English period. Had the aisle been built 50 years later the pillars would have been slimmer and would not dominate the nave as they do now. By the time the present chancel arch was built in the fourteenth century the pointed arch had reached its full stress-bearing potential and a wide arch giving greater access to the chancel was possible. The chancel was totally rebuilt and the vestry added in the nineteenth century. The church contains a large amount of old woodwork, much of it in good condition. The rood screen is fifteenth century and in excellent condition. The rood beam above is not ancient and is probably a copy of the original. The pulpit dated 1628 is decorated with pokerwork patterns. Hanging in the tower is a fine seventeenth century wooden bier. By 1600 coffin burials were becoming the norm and every church possessed a bier to transport the coffin. A surprising number survive today, but this wooden one is one of the best. The fifteenth century font is situated in the south aisle and is decorated with rosettes, a design that was to become more fashionable a century later. The south doorway and porch are sixteenth century and there is an interesting example of a holy water stoup on the outside of the porch. The porch and half the roof are covered with Horsham slabs. The exterior of the church is covered in thick white stucco much as it would have been in ancient times and with its tall broach spire and well-tended churchyard the whole setting is very picturesque. There are a few early eighteenth century gravestones to be found in the interesting churchyard.

COLDWALTHAM *St Giles* ❀ ⌖ 📖 (WSSA)105

Like so many other churches in Sussex the site chosen for the first church at Coldwaltham was close to the Roman road known as the Stane Street. Long after the Romans had departed these isles their straight (Street) stone (Stane) roads were the only real roads in England and continued to be used by all kind of travellers from pilgrims to armies for centuries. There is good evidence of a Saxon church on the site in the form of an ancient coffin lid found in the churchyard (now in the belfry) and possibly the font which may be tenth century. Literally adding considerable weight to the Saxon church theory is the ancient yew tree in the churchyard. Known to be the worshipping places of pagan religions the early church builders often built their churches close to these trees to encourage the congregation into the new religion. The yew here has been dated at over three thousand years old, is one of the ten oldest in the country, and was a giant long before Christ was born. The oldest parts of the church today are the early thirteenth century south aisle and the tower arch. The least altered part is the fourteenth century Early English tower. The tower's half timbered bell stage is much later but suits it very well. In medieval times Coldwaltham was never a rich parish with a manor house to lavish improvements on the church (the very name means 'Cold hamlet on the heath') and for centuries the church was in bad repair. In the eighteenth century it was necessary to rebuild the chancel and replace the pews, some of which remain today. By the nineteenth century the congregation (described at the time as 'all poor agricultural workers') had grown so large they were overflowing into the chancel. Here they sat on benches and even the altar steps and in 1870 the church was enlarged to the north to make more room and most of the interior was replaced at the same time. Of interest from this period are the green and blue tiles round the altar which were made by the famous Minton China Co of Stoke-on-Trent, the fine Tracker-type organ, made by Halmshaw and Sons, Birmingham in 1820, and the stained glass in the north and south aisles. This glass was made by the famous Kempe studios, the glass in the north aisle by Charles Kempe himself and is considered some of his best work. There are some interesting stones in the churchyard and a priest's house nearby, the lower part of which is thirteenth century.

AMBERLEY *St Michael* ❀❀❀ ✠ 📖📖 (WSSA)105

The church at Amberley is joined both historically and physically to Amberley Castle, one of the loveliest and least known castles in southern England. Both castle and church were built around 1100 by Bishop Luffa (builder of Chichester Cathedral) on land granted to St Wilfrid in 670 AD by King Caedwalla. The castle remained the seasonal home of the bishops of Chichester until the sixteenth century and the church prospered from its association. Much of the nave is from the early Norman church but the tower and south aisles were added and the chancel greatly enlarged in 1230 by Bishop Ralph Neville. Bishop Neville was Chancellor of the Realm at that time and the huge chancel reflects the important ceremonies it would have been necessary for him to hold at this church from time to time. A line in the stonework marking the point of the old chancel east wall is clearly visible from the outside. The impressive east window is formed by a group of three typical Early English lancet windows. The original Norman north door is now blocked and the twelfth century font is much restored, but the superb three-order chancel arch remains in all its Norman glory. The early thirteenth century wall paintings are in fair condition and various painted fish can be seen in the yellow borders. Also painted on the nave walls are two consecration crosses. In most churches these crosses (which marked the various stages of the service to consecrate the nave) have almost always been lost over the centuries and the ones that do survive are usually cut into the stone outside the church. In the south aisle is an excellent brass, dated 1424; it shows a man in armour covered by a surcoat. The engraving on the surcoat has been filled with pitch to make it stand out. There is a fine pulpit and near it the original hourglass stand is fixed to the wall, it holds a finely crafted hourglass from the late sixteenth century. The current main door is in the south wall and dates from about 1360. Just to the left of the porch is the oldest stone in the churchyard, dated 1700. The churchyard is large and follows the curtain wall of the castle. Bishop Rede added this fortified wall to the castle in 1380 at a time when French raids reached as far up the river as Amberley. The setting of St Michael's is near perfect with the castle on one side and the picturesque village of thatched houses on the other, all looking out over the Arun Valley.

GREATHAM ❀ ✠✠ 📖 (WSSA)105

If you want to see a good example of a simple single cell church that is much as it was when built then take a look at Greatham. Built around 1100 along with two other churches in the area, all three probably served a community of shepherds in what is still today a marshy, thinly populated part of the county. The layout of the church is primitive even by eleventh century standards; the south wall is longer than the north and the east wall over 30cm longer than the west. The result being that none of the walls meet at a right angle, none are parallel and no two walls are the same thickness, yet all four are original. Even the materials used are a random mix of ironstone, greenstone, chalk, flint and even re-used Roman bricks. As early as 1443 the church shared a priest with nearby Wiggonholt, a common practice today but much rarer then. The shape of the now blocked-up original east window can still be seen as can at least one blocked doorway. Most of the present windows date from the thirteenth century. The only real changes came in the nineteenth century when the bell turret was replaced with a spire, the old porch was replaced with the one we see today and a vestry was added in the north wall. The vestry seems to have been a poor addition and fell down of its own accord in 1950. Under the vestry five uncoffined burials were found; these are thought to be soldiers killed during a small civil war battle at the nearby Greatham Bridge. Inside the church is an interesting and quite rare double-decker pulpit and a good communion rail dating from the mid-1600s. The king post roof is old but not thought to be original. The large 'Sussex marble' slab in the porch may well be a former altar. Three crudely carved crosses to be found on the sandstone quoins are almost certainly 'consecration crosses' put there at the time of the church's building and blessed by the priest sent to consecrate the new church. Even to this day the church has no running water and no electricity and is lit by oil lamps and candles. It is about as basic a church as there is in the southern counties, and none the worse for that.

HARDHAM *St Botolph* ❀❀ ⴲⴲ 📖📖 (WSSA)85

St Botolph's sits in a picturesque setting just off the main road, with a few equally pretty cottages on either side. In medieval times most churches had their walls rendered in white plaster and here at Hardham is as good an example of this kind of exterior as you will find and it certainly adds to the look of the church. Much of the church has definite Saxon characteristics, long and short work, and very tall walls and it probably dates from the late Saxon period, about 1050, as the walls are much thicker than early Saxon examples. The blocked door in the south wall could well be the original Saxon entrance. The Roman 'Stane Street' passed very close and there was a large Roman army base situated nearby. Examination of the walls shows a good deal of Roman tiles and bricks culled from the deserted army camp and used as easy building material. The remaining Early English lancet windows suit the church very well but the later sixteenth century windows add nothing and look a little out of place. Visible on the outside of the south wall is a blocked 'squint' which originally gave a view of the altar from an anchorite's cell which protruded from the south wall. Many churches claim to have had an anchorite cell but few can show any proof but here at Hardham it is known for certain that at least one person, Prior Robert, occupied the cell there until his death in 1285. On the inside the church is dominated by a virtually complete series of wall paintings. Dated about 1100 these are believed to be the earliest in the country and are too numerous to list here but a good guide to the paintings is available in the church. Two of particular interest are the famous 'Adam and Eve' in the chancel and the 'legend of St George' low down on the north wall. If painted in 1100 this latter series, which shows the Saint at the Battle of Antioch in 1098, would be a very early reference to St George who did not become popular in England until after the crusades. Also of interest inside the building are the communion rail, dated 1720, which is in excellent condition, and the bells, one dated 1636 and the other undated but thought to be twelfth century and perhaps the oldest in Sussex. The churchyard contains a few interesting stones including one military marker for a military policeman killed in World War II.

WIGGONHOLT ❀ ✠✠ 📖📖📖 (WSSA)106

Wiggonholt is one of a number of small single cell churches built in this area to serve the shepherds working on the marshy 'Brooks' near Pulborough. Built perhaps a little later than the others in the late twelfth or early thirteenth century it remains unchanged except for the windows which are for the most part in the Perpendicular style of the early fifteenth century. On high ground and surrounded by trees the churchyard is overgrown for much of the year. The tiniest of brooks runs down the outside of the boundary wall to the marshland below. All this makes for a particularly natural and peaceful setting. Inside the simple style is repeated with only a massive Norman font of Sussex marble and a complete set of commandment and creed boards worthy of note. For those interested in seeing the different styles of church roofs it is worth comparing the tie-beam style used here with the kingpost style used at the similar single cell church at nearby Greatham, a church which shared its priest with Wiggonholt as long ago as 1443. Like Greatham there is no electricity here and services have a marvellous ancient atmosphere lit as they are in these churches by candles and oil lamps. There are some old stones in the churchyard and a particularly good 'mass dial' on the southwest corner of the church. These sundials were used in medieval times to time correctly the sections of the mass, a stick being inserted to form the 'gnomon' or indicator. There is a simple bell turret with a nice weather vane.

STORRINGTON *St Mary* (WSSA)107

The former Norman nave is now the north aisle and retains its metre thick walls on the north and east sides. The thirteenth century chancel arch is still in its original position but now leads to the Early English style Lady Chapel, which stands where the chancel used to be. One blocked Norman door can still be seen in the aisle north wall. The arcade on the north side was added in the fifteenth century. In 1745 part of the ancient tower collapsed following poor repair work taking a portion of the nave with it, and in 1750 the tower and nave were rebuilt. Few towers were built at that time and this one is an interesting example. It has a peel of six bells, five of which were cast in 1760, but there must have been older bells in the first tower as one of the clappers dated 1275 was found in the churchyard where it had lain since the collapse. In 1843 the nave and chancel were rebuilt and for some reason largely rebuilt again in 1876. The font is a much-travelled one. It was moved around the church several times following the nave collapse because its original position was open to the elements for some time following the disaster. During the 1843 re-build it was sent to Coolham chapel and replaced with a Victorian version but in 1923 the nineteenth century font was given to Henfield church and the old one returned to its rightful place. The eighteenth century charity boards still survive in the tower and there is a small brass dated 1592 in the chancel but the best memorial is a much later one for the Countess of Carnwarth. The churchyard was originally small but was enlarged by the addition of first the village pound (an area where stray or impounded animals were kept by the village council) and a little later the 'pillery' gardens. The latter is not as it would appear the area where the pillory was set up, but in fact the gardens of a house where medicinal pills were made. The pump from the house can still be seen in the churchyard. There are many old gravestones, the oldest is dated 1705 and can be found on the north side of the church.

WEST CHILTINGTON *St Mary* (WSSA)87

In common with many village churches the dedication of this church was lost for perhaps hundreds of years, only re-surfacing when a will dated 1541 came to light. Other records dealing with the churchyard show that at least 3700 people have been buried there over the centuries. Just outside the boundary wall the ancient village stocks and whipping post are on show. The Saxon church at Chiltington mentioned in the Domesday Book almost certainly stood on the site of the present Norman one which was built between 1100 and 1150 in the transitional Norman style. The typical short stocky arcade pillars support the usual slightly pointed arches that are so much a part of the Transitional style. When the seventeenth century galleries were removed in the 1880s along with the box pews the extensive wall paintings were uncovered but were not preserved for another 50 years and the sharp colours have faded somewhat. The paintings in the south aisle are twelfth century, and almost as old as the church, but in places where the plaster has flaked away even earlier simple patterns can be seen underneath the pictorial story telling pictures on the surface. In the nave much of the artwork is thirteenth century, while the painting on at least one pillar and the excellent example in the splay of the north nave window are fourteenth century The chantry chapel to the south of the chancel was added in the fourteenth century. In the south aisle there is a particularly long hagioscope or 'squint', this gave a direct view of the altar to either those officiating at the side altar in the south aisle, or the operator of the sanctus bell, rung at certain times during the mass. This sanctus bell probably still exists as one of the five bells in the spire which was added in 1602. The original bell clappers are on show in the porch, which is perhaps the oldest in Sussex with woodwork thought to be thirteenth century. Also of interest inside the church are the fourteenth century lock and key on display near the squint, the remains of the rood steps at the eastern end of the aisle which led to the rood loft and in the vestry a rare 'dole cupboard'. This type of cupboard was originally used to store charitable gifts of food which were 'doled out' to the poor. This is the where the term 'on the dole' comes from.

THAKEHAM *St Mary* ❀❀ ✠✠ 🕮🕮 (WSSA)87

From its first mention in the Domesday Book until its decline in the late nineteenth century the village was large and important and the size of the church reflects this. The nave and north transept are twelfth century, the nave fifty years older than the transept which was the site of the original tower. The chancel is thirteenth century and in the Early English style with typical lancet windows, deep splayed on the inside to give maximum light. These are repeated throughout the church replacing all but one of the Norman narrow slit windows. What makes this church of special interest is its restoration and enlargement in the early sixteenth century, a period not known for its church improvements. The tower with its 'chicken coop' roof often seen in France but rare in England dates from this time, as does the porch which contains many of its original timbers. Inside the church a great deal of woodwork from the 1500s survives, more than I've ever seen in a single church. The small door to the tower is over 500 years old and still in use. The screen over the tower arch is probably the old rood screen and dates from the Elizabethan period as does the pulpit, the front four or so rows of pews date themselves with their 'Tudor Rose' motif. The font is a century older and made of clunch, a local limestone, and is more elaborate than usual in Sussex where Norman fonts prevail. Most of the memorials are to the Apsley family and range from early brasses, through tombs to memorial plaques. Perhaps the best is an engraved alabaster slab tomb showing a knight in armour with the engraved lines filled with pitch to show them off at their best. There have been some interesting incumbents at St Mary's, Martin, the rector in 1257, attacked a neighbouring vicar with a pitchfork in a dispute over tithe payments and was shot in the chest with an arrow by his victim's followers for his actions (he survived to appear in court). The dedication of this church is very strange; known everywhere as St Mary's (including the Ordnance Survey map) the true dedication is St Peter and St Paul and always has been. There is no record at all of an official re-dedication to St Mary; the name seems to have just come about by local consent.

WARMINGHURST *Holy Sepulchre* ⌖⌖ 📖📖 (WSSA)108

This simple single cell church built around 1220 is no longer used for services and is now in the hands of The Churches Conservation Trust. The main body of the church is very simple and plain, there is a good thirteenth century east window and a roundel-type window of the same date in the west wall. Most of the other windows have been refurbished with brickwork probably in the seventeenth century, when the brick south porch was added. The two doors to this porch, which opened east and west, are now blocked and entrance to the church is via the west door. The redundant porch does serve to protect the fine south doorway, which must have been the main entrance for many years. The main feature of the church is its interior woodwork, which is in fine repair. The three-decker pulpit,once common place, with its pulpit, clerk's desk and priest's prayer seat is a rare find today. Of the pine pews the front two are clearly squires' pews with two gentleman farmers pews behind those. The excellent screen is the only divide between the nave and chancel. All the woodwork, with the exception of the seventeenth century altar rails, was added around 1770. The extravagant royal arms on the tympanum above the screen are those of Queen Anne as used by her after the combining of England and Scotland in 1707. The font is a small seventeenth century version with an interesting (and very rare) wrought iron 'font crane' above it for lifting the cover. One of the six coloured internal consecration crosses which marked the stations used by the priest who first consecrated the church after it was built survives on the east wall south of the window. The most important memorial in the church is a large brass to Edward Shelley (ancestor of the poet) and his wife, dated 1544. Note the date of his wife's death as Feb 1544/5; this double date is due to the difference of opinion on when New Year's day fell at that time. There are a few old stones in the churchyard including one to Nicholas Shelley, park keeper to the Butler family for forty-seven years, who died in 1756. Although he appears to have had no connection with this church it is interesting to note that William Penn wrote the first constitution for the state of Pennsylvania while living in Warminghurst. Preserved in Lewes is an order for his arrest issued in 1684 for 'holding unlawful assemblies of two hundred people at his house in Warminghurst in contempt of the King and his laws'.

CHURCH WINDOWS

As we have seen earlier no church remains unchanged and the features that change most often are the windows. It is not uncommon to find a church with windows from at least four different periods spanning hundreds of years, all still intact and in use, Eastergate is a good example. Even the very function of windows has changed over the centuries.

The earliest church windows to be found today are Saxon. They are short, narrow and often high up. Their purpose had more to do with letting out smoke than letting in light. There were two main reasons why the Saxon stonemasons kept their windows small. First the wind and rain had to be kept out, glass was expensive or not available at all so windows had to be small. Second the church was often used as a refuge in times of conflict and small castle-like windows were ideal in those circumstances. The best surviving Saxon window is at Poling, found blocked up in the 1920s still with its wooden shutter attached. Several other Sussex churches have good pre-Conquest windows; some re-using Roman tiles to form the heads (Arlington).

With the coming of the Normans in 1066 church design became heavier and more solid but if anything windows got smaller. There were definitely more of them and they did tend to be slightly taller than their predecessors but they were very narrow, the reasons were the same as before. A great many early Norman windows can still be found, notably at Chithurst, Itchingfield and North Marden.

About 1150 things began to change dramatically, the big drawbacks to larger windows were beginning to disappear. Chains of Norman castles were protecting the land (not always successfully), glass was more readily available and advances in architectural design developed the pointed arch, relieving the stresses in door, arcade and window openings, paving the way for larger windows giving more light. This first stage of this Gothic style is called the Early English period and it lasted from 1150 to 1270; a time of much church building in Sussex. The hallmark of this period is the tall, pointed lancet window so common in the county. Builders soon found that the great strength of this kind of window gave it great versatility and it can be found, used as singles or in sets of up to seven. At Stedham there is a beautiful set of five stepped lancets forming the east window. There are a great number of perfect examples of the lancet style of window in the county but for me the simple single lancets in the nave and two wide spaced, deeply splayed east lancets at Barlavington are among the best. They give the smaller village church far more majesty than the grander windows that were to come later.

The next gothic stage was the Decorated period 1270-1370. The windows of this era are much wider and contain large amounts of intricate stone tracery to give strength and divide up the glass panels. Glass was still difficult to make in large sections and expensive so each panel was small and easily replaced. The basic design of the earlier lancet can still be seen incorporated in the larger windows of this time. The east windows at Coldwaltham and Ford are good examples. This style of window lends itself to the use of stained glass, which started to become popular in areas where it could be afforded.

The final stage of the Gothic age is the Perpendicular period (1370-1650). Here the curved tracery has given way to straight stone divides, giving even greater strength and allowing for huge very tall windows. Although a copy, the east window at Horsham is a fine example as are the original windows at Westbourne. Stained glass was in its element with these windows and the actual window decoration is often overshadowed by the glass within it.

In the late seventeenth and eighteenth century glass again became expensive and the stonework of windows became heavier and squarer, the window often only having two lights. At Coombes the west window is a good eighteenth century example. Many church windows were replaced by the Victorians but even they with their love of anything new could not improve on their predecessors and usually replaced in the Decorated or Perpendicular style.

One odd type of window deserves a paragraph all of its own, the low sided window. No other church feature has caused so much debate over its function. At least six different theories have been advanced over the years yet no written reference has ever been found in church records as to its true use. Usually low in the south chancel wall it can also be found in the west and north walls but never in the east. Although not often reported it can also be found high up in the west (Findon) or south wall. Theories include a confessional opening, a vent for incense fumes, even the symbolic site of the spear wound in Christ's side while on the Cross (this fits in with the idea that a church is laid out in the shape of Christ on the Cross). The most common and intriguing idea is that it was a window for lepers to observe the Mass from outside the building. Experts now agree that this is not an option, lepers would not have been allowed onto church ground and this is documented. More evidence against this theory is the existence of examples high in the walls as mentioned earlier. It is generally agreed today that the low sided window was used for the ringing of the Sanctus bell at the high point of the Mass allowing people unable to attend the service to observe the elevation of the host at the correct time. The evidence for this theory is substantial, the window's position on the south side inevitably faces the local village, in instances where the church was unusually built with the village to the north the window is on the north side. The high versions of the window clearly give better range to the sound of a bell and many still contain Sanctus bells. The windows always open inwards allowing them to be opened only when needed and they are always situated where an acolyte seated inside the window could observe the action taking place at the altar. There is, in fact, very often a stone seat by the inside sill. Possibly the sudden removal of the mass from the church following the Reformation caused all mention of the window's use to be shunned as being part of Popish ceremony. With the increase of research into church records perhaps one day written evidence of their real use will surface. Many low sided windows still remain in Sussex, good examples can be seen at Botolphs, Edburton and Lancing.

THE SURREY BORDER

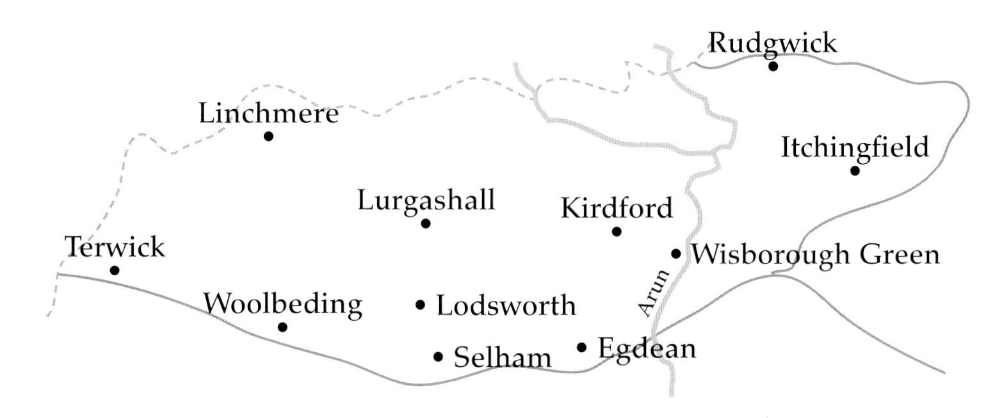

In Norman times the forest here was the densest in England, the population small and the churches few and spread out. Terwick, Rudgwick and Linchmere all hug the Surrey border north of the old forest. Kirdford and Wisborough Green have taken advantage of the nearby river and grown large while Egdean and Woolbeding are still deep in the woods. Itchingfield with its priest's house and wooden tower holds pride of place.

TERWICK *St. Peter*   (WSSA)56

St. Peter's, known as the Church in the Field, is situated on National Trust property, about 200 metres south of the A272, east of Rogate. It is assumed that the church was built as a central focus for a scattered farming community around 1140 and the dedication for St. Peter was adopted during the sixteenth century. There is evidence to suggest that the site may have been a pre-Christian burial ground.

The original Norman church, built mainly of stone rubble, was extensively renovated during the nineteenth century, but the west wall still remains virtually unaltered with the doorway arch, the arch above the door and a small window. The door is not original although the original hinges are thought to have been reused on the new oak door. The belfry is also a modern replacement and contains one bell made by Pack & Chapman in 1774.

The two lancet windows in the nave south wall are of different ages. The one by the font is nineteenth century whilst the one at the chancel end and the one in the south wall of the chancel itself are thirteenth century, but much restored. The east window was erected in 1855 to the memory of the Lyon family.

Also in the south wall of the chancel is what looks like a priest's door but is in fact an original square window which was extended to ground level around 1800.

The large window in the north wall was inserted about 1450 and although the other lancet windows here appear to be thirteenth century they are modern replacements in the Early English style. Internally, there is a single old tie beam in the nave roof and the communion rail is early seventeenth century. The font is Norman but much altered. A small tablet in the church records six men killed in the Great War, one of whom is buried in the churchyard.

Of interest in the churchyard are the ancient stone cross, opposite the west door, and the tomb of John Carnegie (d1892), his wife Charlotte and their daughter Mary (d1854). John was the son of William Carnegie, the 7th Earl of Northesk, who was third in command at the Battle of Trafalgar.

LINCHMERE *St Peter* ❀❀ ✠✠ 📖📖 (WSSA)16

The parish of Linchmere borders both Surrey and Hampshire and its church stands over five hundred feet above sea level, offering perhaps the longest views of any church in Sussex. The outside of the building is rather plain, with the entire north side having been rebuilt after 1856. Inside there is quite a change, with items of interest on every side. Much of the old two cell Saxon church can be seen on the south side including the very interesting original west door which now leads to the vestry. The doorway is certainly Saxon but fairly late, as it is rebated which is rare for Saxon work. As with many early churches the building was clearly a place of refuge and the slots to take a huge wooden lock bar can be seen in the doorjambs. The original church was only about seven metres long and the tall thin walls and long and short work show that the south wall at least is original. The Normans seem to have enlarged the church to the east in three stages, the boundaries of which can be seen from the changes in the base plinth. The first change around 1100 would have been the removal of the apse and squaring off of the eastern end, about 100 years later the chancel was enlarged again to the east and shortly after that in about 1240 the final eastern extension was added. Due to the devastation caused by the Black Death in 1348 it wasn't until the tower was added to replace the ancient wooden turret in the eighteenth century that further enlargement was needed. (The sundial on the south side, although dated 1654, was not originally on the tower). One of the two bells is thought to be over 700 years old. By 1800 the village had grown and the chancel was again enlarged and shortly after in 1856 a north aisle was added. Fifty years later another north aisle was built on, giving the church its present lopsided appearance. Features of interest inside the church are the twelfth century font and the fourteenth century stone carvings of the seven deadly sins on the north wall. These are in the form of monks and were carved about 1300 in Italy and brought to the church in 1906. Close examination of the window in the children's corner shows a medieval head built into the modern window.

WOOLBEDING *All Hallows (aka All Saints)* ❀❀ ✠✠ (WSSA)58

All Hallows is a dedication often associated with Saxon churches and that holds true here. The nave with its high, thin walls and pilaster strips on both north and south sides was probably built about 1050 and is from the same church mentioned in the Domesday Book nine hundred years ago. What appears to be a blocked priest's door in the nave wall started life as a low sided window and was extended down to floor level before finally being blocked up. No other building features from the Saxon or Norman period remain and the only other items at all that can claim any great age are the plain twelfth century tub-shaped font and a thirteenth century stone coffin lid still in situ in the church floor. There are some particularly good sixteenth century Flemish stained glass panels, these were originally made for the chapel of the Holy Ghost in Basingstoke. From the seventeenth century come the set of commandment boards and two bells dated 1665 and 1616. The present tower was added in 1728 and the old reredos now on the south wall of the chancel is of the same period. There are several eighteenth century memorials inside the church but none as interesting as the large memorial to Capt. J. Dodsworth (d1773) in the churchyard. This has military scenes depicted on its sides and is a very early example of its kind. The church must have once stood in the grounds of nearby Woolbeding House and is to this day surrounded by its grounds on three sides. This makes for a very pleasant setting indeed.

LURGASHALL *St Laurence* ❀❀ ✠✠✠ 📖 (WSSA)38

The setting at Lurgashall is easy to imagine, for it is the typical picture postcard Sussex village. The church is tucked in the corner of the large village green with the village inn for its nearest neighbour. Almost certainly on the site of the first wooden Saxon church the present building contains considerable signs of Saxon work. The tall nave with herringbone stonework in both north and south walls is certainly pre-Conquest, but perhaps not from the first stone church thought to have been built as early as the seventh century. The thirteenth century tower is unusually situated in the south wall and originally had a wooden spire (added in the fifteenth century) this was removed in the 1950s and replaced with the present one some years later. There are two mass dials scratched into the tower (south and east) and one remaining 'consecration cross' (south). The unique cloister on the south wall was built in the sixteenth century as a resting place for travellers passing through on the old Roman road and was enclosed in 1622 to form a school and village meeting place, the rare woodwork dates from this time. In the porch can be seen a very rare 'resurrection stone'; these were rented out to be placed on top of new graves to prevent grave robbers stealing corpses for dissection. The church seems to have more history linked to the English Civil War than most and its connections with both sides through Cromwell himself and the Yaldwyn family seems to have kept the village out of the fighting, but the marks of unrest remain. The list of rectors shows the sudden arrival of Cromwell's puritan man and his just as sudden removal on the King's restoration. The old font, broken by puritans, can be seen in the porch and the new one, dated 1662 and first used on Lady Day of that year following the reintroduction of the baptism service, is just inside the church. There are a few small fragments of wall paintings from the fifteenth century and a very impressive wall clock, this type of clock is called an 'act of parliament clock'. A little searching will reveal two church chests from the seventeenth and eighteenth centuries.

LODSWORTH *St Peter* ❀❀ ✠ (WSSA)60

Only the tower survives from the early church at Lodsworth. The rest of the building was rebuilt in the late nineteenth century in that curious Victorian style that tried to copy medieval architecture but always appears as clearly Victorian. The tower however is a gem and worth a visit on its own. Built in the fourteenth century it has remained largely untouched and is an excellent example of its period. The great west door with its typical pointed arch was clearly the main entrance to the old church and still retains the damaged remains of a water stoup at its side. Another good example of its kind is the pyramidal 'Sussex cap', which protects the tower. Throughout Great Britain many methods of roofing towers have been tried but I believe these caps, synonymous with Sussex, work the best. Their success could well be the reason why Sussex has so many medieval towers still standing, often when the rest of the church has been rebuilt. The cap at Lodsworth is shallow and slightly overhangs the tower offering additional protection to the walls. Inside the church the tower has more to offer with its arch resting directly on the tower east walls rather than using imposts. The main roof beams were reused from the old church. There are some eighteenth century grave slabs in the floor and some nice, if not a little uncomfortable, box pews but almost everything else is less than 150 years old. The church sits close to the manor house in a near perfect setting, with extensive views to the north east and a formidable stone boundary wall protecting the rather small churchyard. There are a few very old stones, some in very good condition dating from 1726 and there is a large and unusual double-arched grave marker on the east side, which although not very old is quite unique and deserves a little restoration.

SELHAM *St James* ❀ ✠✠✠ 📖📖📖 (WSSA)82

This tiny church is surely one of the most interesting in southern England. The basic structure contains a great deal of unaltered Saxon work, perhaps over 1000 years old. Although the Normans must have had a lot to do with the church we see today they seem to have left the structure they inherited in 1066 much as it was before the Conquest. The tall thin walls built in the herringbone style could be used as a benchmark for identifying Saxon church architecture and the size and layout follows closely that used by St Wilfrid when building churches during his conversion of Sussex. The eighteenth century north porch protects the original Saxon door, once again a perfect example of its kind. Round-arched and less than a metre wide it is still the only entrance to the church, so by stepping across the threshold you are following in the footsteps of thousands of worshippers from Saxon and Norman times through Tudor and Georgian to Victorian and the present day. Inside the church the first thing to strike you is the huge Norman font, clearly from the days when total immersion was still the fashion. The marks of the tools used in its making can still be seen on the outside and date the font to about 1100. Turning to face the altar the church's most outstanding feature is revealed in all its glory. The chancel arch is second to none, although the arch itself is Norman work it blends in perfectly with the older Saxon parts. The capital on the south side shows a snake devouring its own tail, while to the north another serpent faces west. These serpent motifs are common on Saxon chancel arches and always face west, away from the sacred eastern end of the church. The impost on the north side is thought to be a piece from a Roman building reused by the Saxon mason. On the south side even the mortar is the original Saxon mix and can be seen to contain cow hairs and crushed tiles, probably also from a Roman building. The south aisle was added in the fourteenth century and its arch is a good example of how improved design allowed for a larger arch than the early chancel one. The particularly good Victorian stained glass is interesting for its subject matter.

EGDEAN *St Bartholomew* ❀ ⴱⴱ (WSSA)84

The old church that originally stood on this secluded spot had fallen into ruin by the mid-sixteenth century and rather than restore the building it was pulled down. At that time, not long after the Reformation, when there were more churches than priests to work them, this was the fate of many churches in poorly populated areas. In 1622 a new church was built, a very quiet time for church building despite the biggest population boom since the Conquest and it is rare to find one in Sussex, as there were so many ancient churches waiting to serve the new congregations. Although mostly built in the Traditional manner a new material was becoming popular in the seventeenth century, brick, and it was used to some effect at Egdean. One small window in the west wall, the internal surrounds of the chancel windows, the main doorway and the chancel arch all contain the small dark bricks of the time. The doorway bears the date 1622 and the chancel arch has been little altered since it was built. It is true that there has been extensive restoration in the last one hundred years but the rare brickwork and the period from which the church dates make it well worth a visit. All the windows, with the possible exception of the previously mentioned one in the west wall, are modern. The font and many of the roof beams are contemporary with the building of the church; one of the beams actually bears the date 1623. There are some nice carved eighteenth century gravestones in the churchyard and one military marker near the porch for a member of the RAF dated 1941. The bell which is clearly visible to the eye and the elements, in its modern bellcote was originally cast in 1737, but was re-cast to mark the Royal Silver Jubilee in 1935 and is inscribed to that effect.

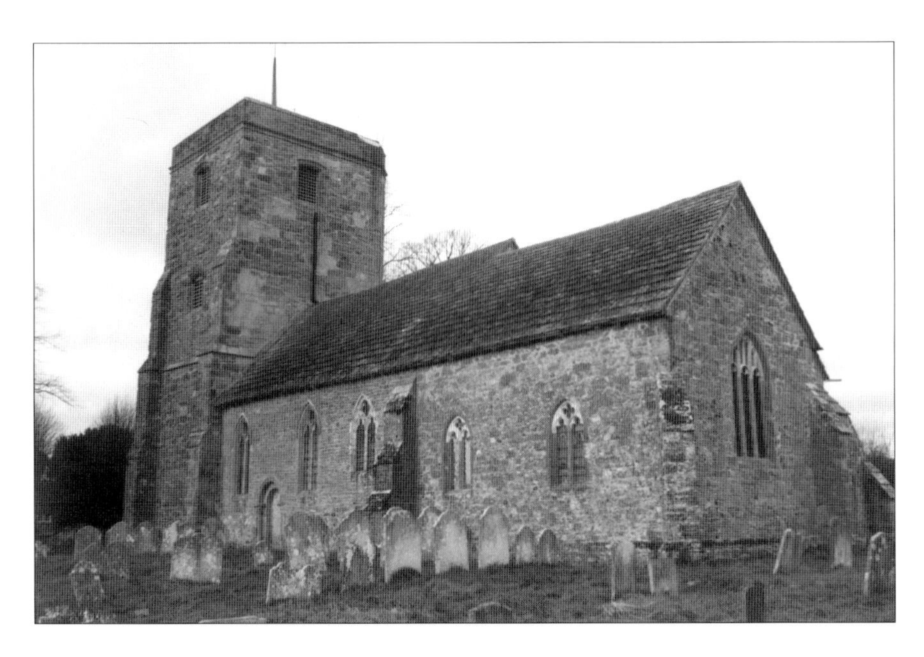

KIRDFORD *St John the Baptist* ❀ ✠✠ 📖 (WSSA)41

The parish of Kirdford was for centuries the largest in West Sussex and was famous for its glass factories and Sussex marble quarries. One north lancet window contains fifteenth century glass from a local works and the font, dated 1620 was, like many others in the county, made from Kirdford marble.

The oldest surviving parts of the church are the early twelfth century south doorway (blocked), part of the west wall (interior) and the herringbone stonework in the south nave wall. In the thirteenth century the north wall was replaced by a fine arcade of three Early English arches leading to a north aisle wide enough to almost double the width of the nave. This aisle went the full length of the church at that time, but the chancel was extended further east a short time later. The east window of the aisle is contemporary with the aisle whereas the east window in the chancel is a fifteenth century addition. During the building of the aisle a small vaulted sacristy or treasury was added to the north of the chancel, the iron nail-studded oak door to the sacristy is probably original. The stocky tower was built in the fifteenth century and originally had a vaulted room at ground level, the remains of the ceiling struts with human and animal head corbels can still be seen at its edges. There are two ancient doors in the tower. These are the west door, which contains old ironwork from the days before the tower was built when it was in the west wall of the church, and the very interesting newel staircase door which retains its ancient lock box and ten iron bands. The woodwork forming the front part of the ringer's gallery is sixteenth century. Other interesting woodwork consists of the twelve benches with carved benchends in the north aisle and the communion rail, which like so many others is early eighteenth century. This is because the rails were removed by law in 1641 but allowed back into churches after the Restoration of Charles II. The west porch still has late medieval woodwork in its upper stages and Elizabethan balusters supported on a brick base.

WISBOROUGH GREEN *St Peter ad Vincula* ❀❀ ⌖⌖ 📖 (WSSA)42

The church sits on top of a steep round, possibly man-made hill and some experts believe the square west end of the church may have been a defensive keep before being reused as part of a Norman church. Whatever the ancient history of the site there was certainly a church here by 1150 and parts of the nave walls and the previously mentioned west end remain. The font is very early thirteenth century and the excellent wall painting in a recess left of the Early English chancel arch is of the same date. It shows the crucifixion below and St James the Great above. St James was a popular saint with pilgrims and the church would have been on a pilgrim route to Chichester, the site of St Richard's shrine. The aisles were added about 1250 but both had been rebuilt within 100 years. During this fourteenth century refit the roof was raised and the rows of clerestory windows added. The now inaccessible rood loft entrance remains high up to the north of the chancel arch. The large size of the western end of the nave and the offset tower leaves plenty of room for a raised organ loft, which hints at an earlier music gallery to the northwest. The stone south porch and the timber north porch are both fifteenth century, the north retaining a large amount of the original woodwork. There are also two old pews in the north porch still bearing the names of the farms whose families used them. The ancient stone altar is very rare and may be thirteenth century. This type of altar would have been the standard in all churches prior to the Reformation but all stone altars were ordered to be destroyed by Henry VIII and replaced by wooden tables. This one was saved by becoming the chimney breast of a vicarage being built at the time at nearby Loxwood. During the Second World War many Canadian soldiers were stationed around Wisborough Green and references can be found around the church to those who were killed on the ill-fated Dieppe raid on 19th August 1942. The doors to the bellringing chamber are dedicated to their memory. The churchyard has a few ancient stones and extensive views of the Downs, a very pleasant spot in the summer but it can be harsh in the winter.

RUDGWICK *Holy trinity* ❀❀ ✠✠ (WSSA)23

The church stands at the northern end of the village, so close to Surrey that the county boundary path cuts through the churchyard. Over the centuries local rivalry from either side of the border over the position of the boundary developed into a traditional good-natured 'fight' each Whit Monday. The oldest stonework is perhaps in the south nave wall, which was rebuilt in the fourteenth century using the stones from the twelfth century Norman original. The short solid tower is the church's best external feature, it was added in the early thirteenth century using large stones making the walls over 1.5 metres thick. Between its tall clasping buttress is set a fine west door with a three-light fourteenth century window above. Higher still are an original belfry opening, a clock and a nice Sussex cap to top it off. In the nave a fourteenth century north aisle is accessed though an arcade of pillars and arches in the more complex style that was beginning to replace the plainer Early English period of a hundred years earlier. The east window has been rebuilt (at least on the outside) but the tall nave windows contain early examples of the additional tracery that was to became the hallmark of the Perpendicular architectural period (1350-1530). There is a piscina and aumbry in the chancel, the latter is considered a good example of its kind. The font is older than the rest of the building, its base dating from the early twelfth century. Much of the church interior was replaced during the extensive nineteenth century restoration.

Bells seem to have featured large in the church history. As long ago as 1521 several bequests are listed for their maintenance and purchase. In the eighteenth century the bells were re-cast into a set of six new bells and a painting on a plaster panel (re-covered from a nearby inn) depicts their first peal on July 27th 1770. Of the eight bells in the tower today three are from the 1770 set, two of which have been re-cast. The churchyard has some interesting grave markers and good views into both Surrey and Sussex.

ITCHINGFIELD *St Nicolas* ❀ ✝✝ 📖📖 (WSSA)44

Of the Norman church built in 1125 only the nave's north and west walls survive. The latter retains the original main church door. The door, which is said to have still its Norman hinge hangers, is now the door to the tower. There is no chancel arch between nave and chancel although there is a screen, a recent re-build using wood from the fifteenth century screen. The roof was boarded in, but was uncovered in the nineteenth century when a human skull was found on top of one of the beams. The fourteenth century west window, which used to look onto the outside world, has for the last 500 years looked into the church's finest feature, its wooden tower. Surprisingly for an area that had the densest forest in England this is the only 100% wooden tower in the county. Built in the fifteenth century entirely of oak it rests on four 60cm square beams each made from a whole tree, four giant uprights are cross-braced and the gaps panelled. The whole tower is held together with oak pins. It has two wooden staircases one of which is ancient. It has a wood-framed window facing the one in the church west wall. The tower is free-standing and not attached to the church at all. A fact which became apparent in the early twentieth century when someone who thought they knew better than the fifteenth century builders removed two of the braces to give better access to the staircase only to find the tower rocked alarmingly when the bells were rung. A certain Mr Parker quickly installed the necessary replacements. As you leave the church take note of the printed list on the back of the main door. It defines which family members it is not legal or morally correct to marry each other. This eighteenth century list must be the last vestige of the 'blood book' which in the small closely related communities of medieval times the priest consulted to check how closely a couple were related before giving his blessing to a marriage. In the churchyard is the church's other treasure, its priest's house. Built in the fifteenth century to house the visiting priest from Sele priory, it was extended to the west about a century later. In later years it saw service as a poor house and vestry and now in retirement is somewhat of a tourist attraction.

ARUNDEL TO WORTHING

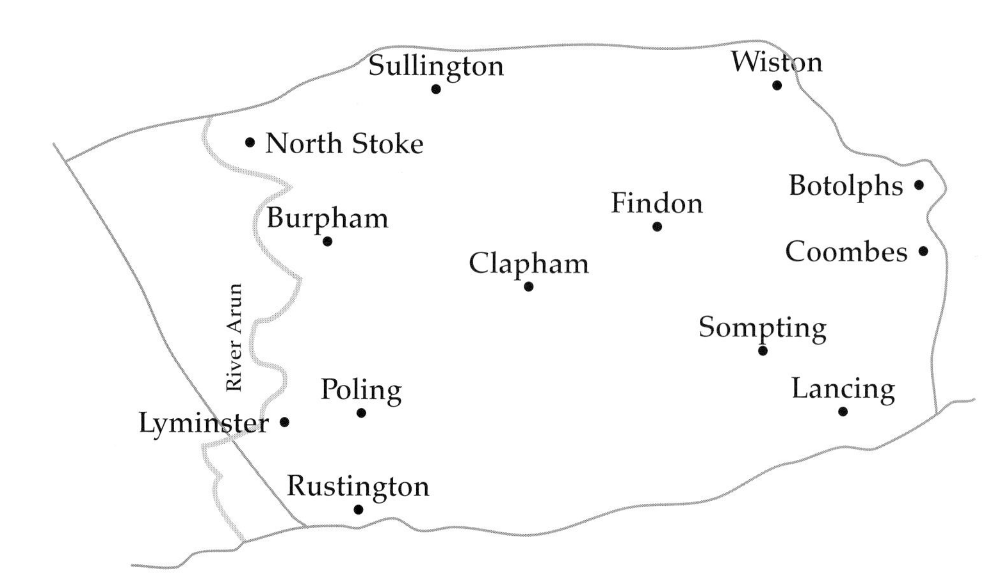

Between the Arun and the Adur lies a fertile coastal plain, heavily populated in the south and wooded in the north. To the west ancient Burpham looks across the river to younger Arundel. Saxon Poling should not be missed and isolated North Stoke is unique. In the east Sompting's Dutch capped tower is the best feature while once-important Botolphs and tiny Coombes cling to the Adur's west bank.

NORTH STOKE ❀❀ ⌖⌖⌖ 🕮 (WSSA)125

This church is now in the hands of The Churches Conservation Trust and services are rarely held there. It sits within a pre-Christian earthwork at the very end of a long narrow lane that follows the eastern bank of the river Arun from Houghton Bridge. Almost unchanged for over 700 years the church is famous for its various windows which clearly show the development of church window design from early Norman slit lancets through Early English tall lancets, to the large three-light windows in the north and south transepts. Only the east window is modern and of little interest.

Small for a cruciform church it is made of flint and stone from the nearby fields and although the wall paintings have now almost gone it is brightly coloured as it would have been in medieval times. The north and south transepts were added about 1290 with the north one being reinforced to take a tower, this was never built and a belfry sits awkwardly in its roof. The tall canopied seat in the south transept is very unusual and has a corbel shaped like a sheep's head above it. Other interesting stone supports take the form of two statue holders in the shape of monks heads and a corbel next to the fourteenth century chancel arch carved in the shape of a human hand. This must have been an important church in its day having three altars (the piscina survive from each) and a fine sedilia in the chancel. This three-seat resting place for the clergy clearly shows the hierarchy of religion at the time with the celebrant's seat higher than the dean's which is higher than the sub-dean's. The roof is of a very simple design, which has obviously been successful as many of the beams are over 700 years old. Set in the floor are six large ledger slabs from the seventeenth and early eighteenth centuries that probably took the places previously held by the three ancient stone coffin lids which can now be seen in the sparsely populated churchyard. The simple bowl-shaped font sits on a plain narrow pillar and dates from about 1250. A fair amount of rare thirteenth century stained glass has survived although much of it has been cleverly reset.

BURPHAM *The Virgin Mary* ❀❀ ✚✚ 📖 (WSSA)125

The church lies two miles inland from Arundel at the site of a fortification built by King Alfred. The road from Arundel to the church offers superb views across the river to the castle. Most of the north nave wall, including the very small window, is generally thought to be Saxon although so late that the church may have been completed after the Conquest. Cruciform in shape, but lacking the usual central tower, the varying transept arches are some of the church's best features, the north arch viewed from the north side is particularly good. The simple Norman chancel arch was lost during refurbishment in 1800. The transepts were added about 1150 but the south was rebuilt along with the south aisle in 1869. This rebuild was a copy of the original, rare in Victorian times and it works very well. The chancel is perhaps the best feature of all, it certainly catches the eye as soon as you enter the church. Rebuilt in 1190 it has a majestic vaulted roof, the ribs of which spring from unusual corbels. Three widely spaced and deeply splayed original lancets form the east window and add to the grandeur. The glass was made by William Wailes in 1869. Wailes specialised in imitating medieval glass and these east windows are some of his best work. The small opening high in the east wall (best seen from outside) is thought to have been the access to a room above the chancel. The piscina and double aumbry are twelfth century and the side windows fourteenth. The font is fifteenth century, a rare date for a Sussex font, and has rosettes as decoration. Also a Sussex rarity is the west tower, one of the very few fifteenth century towers in the county. I believe the tower was once plastered on the outside as the beam and scaffolding holes are now clearly visible which they surely would not have been when the tower was completed. The three chandeliers date from about 1750, the communion rail is a little earlier. The oldest woodwork is probably the carved bench ends which are the same age as the font and tower. The churchyard is large and has some interesting stones, none more so than one to the right of the porch. It has a carving of a racehorse and rider in full gallop and is for Benjamin Brewster (d1789), a famous jockey of the time.

LYMINSTER *St Mary Magdalene* ❀ ⊕⊕⊕ 📖 (WSSA)145

The first thing to strike you about this church is its size. For a village church it is enormous and has a large churchyard containing many large tombs and old stones. The massive roof is now tiled, but was originally of Horsham stone slabs, these were removed as their weight was endangering the structure. The north aisle roof had already been reinforced in the fifteenth century to give extra support. The original church is believed to have been part of the Saxon Benedictine nunnery that existed to the south of the present church prior to 1000AD. After the Conquest, the nunnery was re-founded as a priory, belonging to the Norman Abbey of Almanesches, only to be dissolved in the late fifteenth century. Both nave and chancel walls date from 1040 at which time the nave was the people's church, while the chancel was the nuns' church, separated by a high wooden partition. The north aisle was added in 1170 and there was a chapel for the use of the nuns, close to where the font now stands. The proportions of the church show its early origins, long and tall. The chancel has been much altered over the years. The Perpendicular east window is early fifteenth century and the large piscina in the south wall is late twelfth century. Opposite, in the north wall, is a large chalk aumbry moved to its present position in the late nineteenth century. The window on the north side appears to be the filling of an archway. The Saxon chancel arch was probably heightened in 1170.

The nave has two lancet windows and on the south side a round window, thought to date from 1260, not an unknown shape but in a very unusual position. Also in the south wall is the blocked Saxon main entrance above the Caen stone Norman doorway (also blocked); both can still be seen when viewed from the outside. The old west doorway now forms the tower arch. The windows in the north aisle are Victorian replacing two square windows and two dormers in the roof. The north porch was added in the fifteenth century, but the gate is a modern addition. The lower tower dates from the thirteenth century, the upper section, including the bell chamber, (the oldest bell dates from 1759) was added in the fifteenth century. The Norman font is late twelfth century, quite plain, made of Sussex marble and lined with lead. Many myths and legends are associated with the area, including dragons and ghosts. There is an intriguing tombstone close to the font for Jim Pulk, the dragon slayer.

POLING *St Nicholas* ❀❀ ✠✠✠ 📖📖📖 (WSSA)146

The church of St Nicolas in the tiny parish of Poling, south of Arundel, is jammed full of interesting features and items accumulated over its one thousand year history and is a church not to be missed. From the first Saxon stone church remain the nave north wall, (with one window), the west part of the north chancel wall (internal) and all four corners of the original nave. The window is remarkable, unblocked in 1917 after six hundred years it still contained its wooden shutter, which is on show below. The south arcade was inserted into the Saxon wall and the aisle built about 1190 by the Knights of St John who had a small priory nearby. They clearly had close links with this church and a coffin lid from one of their tombs can be seen in the chancel. The south arcade has interesting uneven octagonal capitals on the columns, a style only used between 1190 and 1200. About 1390 the tiny Saxon chancel with narrow arch was replaced with the present chancel by extending the nave walls east leaving no divide other than the rood screen and beam. Both of these survive, the former only in part and heavily restored and the latter an ancient replacement from another church (Bargham) The original beam must have been large enough to support a loft for its fifteenth century access doorways, both lower and upper are still in place. Three modern statues stand on fourteenth century image brackets that flank the altar and together with the modern version of an ancient reredos give an excellent impression of what a chancel looked like in medieval times. The nave windows were added around 1420 about the same time as the tower and north doorway (now blocked) were built. The font is Saxon but stands on a fifteenth century base. Next to the door is the only surviving ancient poor box in the county. The top plate is dated 1285 and the front plate 1797,the woodwork is probably of this later date. The churchyard contains some good eighteenth century stones and one interesting modern one. Dated 2000 it is to 'Colin, Lord Cowdrey of Tonbridge' better known as the great England cricketer Colin Cowdrey.

RUSTINGTON *St Peter & St Paul* ❀ ✠✠ 📖 (WSSA)168

The earliest church on the site was built about 1100 and from it small portions of the stonework at each of the four corners of the nave survive. The tower and south arcade are from the Transitional style church, built about 1170, both tower arch and the arcade have typical slightly pointed arches of this period. The arches of the north arcade, built in the Early English style of one hundred years later, clearly show the improvements in design over those to the south. The chancel with its northeasterly inclination was re-built and the north chapel added at the same time as the north aisle. The chapel has a tall arch to the west almost identical to the main chancel arch. On one pillar of this arch portrait masks have been carved into the capitals. Both north and south outer walls are mostly nineteenth century but portions of the old walls remain, especially low down. In the south wall at the eastern end of the nave is a narrow low window which was once the vantage point into the church from a thirteenth century anchorite's cell which shows in drawings of the church from 1780 as a large bulge in the nave wall. The large expanse of wall, with no windows in the north wall opposite, marks the position of another similar cell, the window of which can still be made out in the stonework. The chancel north lancet has fifteenth century glass in the roundels and there is a small priest's door with a well-preserved mass dial on the external eastern jamb. In the chancel there is a good sixteenth century wall tomb showing Richard Covert and his wife kneeling in prayer. The rood loft staircase is rare, in that it was not cut until the fifteenth century, a time when the rood loft and beam were in decline. The church roofs were replaced in the 1800s, the nave with a fine king post version but the chancel has a poor looking roof of Victorian design. The tower would certainly have been the best feature of the church had it not been rendered with cement in 1926. It does retain its original windows, slits low down and double belfry openings above. Inside it one bell dated 1670 remains of the three mentioned in 1720, the bell housing is partly medieval. On show in the tower are the workings of the early one-handed church clock, made in the eighteenth century. Both porches are old, the north one has been almost completely renewed but the west porch retains much of its original fourteenth century woodwork including the bargeboard.

SULLINGTON *St Mary* ❀ ⚲ 📖📖 (WSSA)107

Parts of the tower and chancel can certainly claim to be Saxon but only just, for the stone Saxon church here is thought to have been built about 1050, just 16 years before the Conquest. It is known that at about that time Aelfwine, the King's sheriff for Kent, gave '3 hides of land for his and his wife's soul'. This type of bequest was common at the time, the land being given specifically for the building of a church. The first Norman work wasn't carried out until 1175 when the tower was rebuilt. There is a strange and rare squint behind the pulpit cut directly through a chancel arch column and facing the south nave wall. It has been suggested that this was a leper squint or gave a view of the altar from an anchorite's cell. The anchorite's cell theory would suggest that the cell with its squint was built at the same time as the church or major work was carried out to cut through the pillar at some later stage to accommodate the squint, both of which seem unlikely. Although a nice idea, research in recent years has all but ruled out the existence of purpose-built leper windows and squints. Close examination of the shape of the roof in the nave, together with the angle of the squint would point strongly to the original south nave wall having been some feet further south, with the squint connecting a side altar to the chancel. This change to the nave could have taken place in 1220 when most of the building we see today was built. An unusual memorial is the ornate organ in the short north aisle, which as well as being a fine musical instrument is also a memorial to Clara Palmer, church organist for 50 years. Near the door is a full-length stone effigy of a crusader knight. Almost certainly a member of the De Covert family, his legs are crossed indicating a crusader and indeed a knight with the De Covert name is listed among those at the siege of Acre. Near the fifteenth century font is a stone coffin lid of the same age. In the churchyard there is a fragment of a wooden grave board and some interesting old stones. There are also what might be the remains of a wooden pump and a very interesting war memorial. This memorial is formed from an old stone ground roller and among those listed are the commander and crew of submarine E24. The church setting is very picturesque with what appears to be an Iron Age hill fort off to the south.

Stained glass window, Old Shoreham

Sompting

Stopham

West Chiltington

Chest tombs, Newtimber

Wall paintings, Coombes

Priest's House, Itchingfield

CLAPHAM *St Mary* ❀ ✠ 📖📖 (WSSA)147

The village of Clapham sits a little north of Worthing on the main London road. The church stands at the end of a long unmade road, a considerable distance from the village. Most likely the local lord who may have built the church and received revenue from it wanted it close to his manor or perhaps the village moved. Villages have moved for many reasons over the centuries, the plague, flood, even the whim of the local lord but as usual the church remains in stately isolation.

Of the original Norman church only a blocked window in the north aisle remains and the main fabric of the building is thirteenth century. Of the two aisles the north is clearly the older (but not by much) and belongs more or less to the Transitional period rather than the out and out Early English style of the south aisle. Viewed from the north the church has a very odd profile with the roof sloping low to the south but cut sharply off to the north where the tower integrates itself into the north and west walls. The chancel, like others in the area, inclines more to the north than is usual. Most of the windows are typical Early English lancets but both aisles contain plain two-light windows from the fifteenth century. The lancets on the west side suit the church particularly well, two small ones in the tower, another in the south aisle and three large ones forming the main west window. Inside the church there are signs of nineteenth century restoration particularly to the chancel arch. There are some fine memorials mostly to the Shelley family who were lords of the manor in the sixteenth century. There are several brasses, the best of which is to John Shelley (d 1526) and his wife; also a good example of a canopied wall tomb. This recessed tomb shows William Shelley (d 1548) and his wife kneeling in prayer with their fourteen children. Note that William's wife is positioned in the middle of the line of children as if keeping an eye on them. The oldest memorial is an early stone slab now in the north aisle. The churchyard is sparsely populated now but the ground probably holds hundreds of former parishioners. Churches with complete records often record thousands of burials over the centuries in an area traditionally of just one acre.

FINDON *St John* ❀ ✠ 📖 (WSSA)128

Despite extensive restoration in 1867 some of the walls from the church of 1180 still survive, pierced by successive aisle openings but still visible from the inside. Small areas of what was the south transept of the cruciform-shaped Norman church may even be older than 1180. The church roof is impressive and interesting. Built in the fifteenth century it replaced a smaller roof with lean-to aisle roofs and now covers both nave and aisles in one span. Large tie beams were needed and the king posts sit on the aisle supports giving an impression of a split nave. In the east wall of the transept is an unusual arch narrower at its base than its midpoint. This arch may have been the original chancel arch or led to an apse but now leads to a recess containing a carved boss probably from a crypt roof. The north chapel, tower and present chancel arch are all thirteenth century, as is the old font. The latter is much damaged and was replaced during the nineteenth century re-fit with the one now in use. The bells are of some interest. There are six in all including a sanctus bell housed in the roof above the pulpit with its own opening in the gable. This is a rare high example of the 'low sided' windows usually found in the chancel south wall. The oldest bell is dated 1576 which is in fact the date it was re-cast from an older bell. The inscription contains no less than nine letters either upside down or backwards. This would perhaps indicate an attempt by the bell founder John Cole (who is known to have been illiterate) to use the complicated wax letter method to inscribe the bell. The letters would need to be written backwards in the wax to come out correctly on the bell and he seems to have become completely confused and probably did not understand his mistakes on the finished bell. Interestingly he seems never to have used this method again.

The exterior of the church is mostly uninteresting nineteenth century work but there are good views of the building from the back of the sloping churchyard. There are some early eighteenth century gravestones including a group of well-preserved ones close to the chancel north wall.

WISTON *St Mary* ❀❀ ⴱⴱ 📖📖 (WSSA)129

Wiston church and the old manor, now Wiston House, stand close to each other in stately isolation in the middle of Wiston Park. Almost total rebuilding was necessary in 1862 to save the thirteenth century church after almost two hundred years of neglect. Surviving from the old building are the tower (fourteenth century), part of the north nave, and surprisingly, part of the roof. Both east and west windows were saved and reinserted in the new building although restoration of the east window has been carried out in recent years. The small heraldic stained glass shields set in these windows date from the fourteenth century. Note that those in the east window have been inserted backwards facing out of the church. The churchyard has a large number of old stones set against the boundary wall but is very small in size, pushed as it is up against the manor house. The best memorials are inside the church although all of the really old memorials have suffered considerable damage. There is a very large (1.5 mtr) early fifteenth century brass for Sir John de Braose depicting a knight in armour. Several monuments for the Shirley family, one badly damaged, and a brass, to Ralph Shirley who was esquire to Henry VII. There are several large floor slabs for the Fagge family, one of these carries the date 1700/1. A similar double-date memorial appears at Jevington in East Sussex, These oddities are probably explained by the fact that the date of New Year was in dispute at this time and different views would have placed this man's death in two different years. There is a good example of a canopied wall tomb containing an effigy of a child. The ancient chest is interesting, it is later than most you come across, perhaps sixteenth century and it may be a churchwarden's chest as it only has two locks, although it may have had a third at some time. If it did it would have been a parish chest, one lock for the rector and one each for the churchwardens. At the rear of the nave on the north side five rare sixteenth century benches have survived. Also at the west end, and best viewed from the inside, is a very fine wooden screen incorporated into the main door. Built into this are the royal arms of George III with the date 1795, although the screen is perhaps somewhat earlier. The square Norman font is smaller than usual and in good condition.

SOMPTING *St Mary* ❀❀ ✠✠✠ 📖📖 (WSSA)149

Famous throughout England for its tower St Mary's has many other important architectural features. The tower with its 'Rhenish Helm' cap is unique in England and for many years was thought to be entirely Saxon. Recent work suggests that only the lower part is Saxon and the upper built just after the Conquest either to a Saxon design or simply as a copy of the original. The tower arch is certainly Saxon and is set to one side to allow for the altar that was once in the tower chamber. In 1154 the crusader order known as the Knights Templar was given the church and at once rebuilt the nave and chancel on the same lines as the old Saxon church, resulting in the nave being the same width as the tower. Some Saxon and Norman windows survive and most of the later ones are fifteenth century. The north transept and what is now the south transept were built at the same time as the nave but the south was a completely separate church for the Templars' own use and was not connected to the church until the nineteenth century. The blocked doors that were used to pass between the two buildings can still be seen. Close examination of the area around the twelfth century font shows evidence of the former chancel of this private chapel. There is an excellent Norman carving of an abbot close to the font. The door beyond the font led to a sacristy built as a strong room. The Templars paid no taxes and became super rich, which worried both the Pope and the crowned heads of Europe and was to be their eventual downfall. In a secretly planned operation the great powers of the Christian world, both secular and religious, joined forces and the Templars were virtually wiped out throughout Europe one Friday the 13th in 1306. The belief that Friday the 13th is an unlucky day stems from this action. In 1324, by order of the Pope, the church became the property of the Templars' rival order the Knights of St John who soon added a large chapel north of the tower. In 1540 this order was in turn dissolved by Henry VIII as part of the Reformation and the chapel fell into ruin. Re-founded in 1831 and best known today as the St John's Ambulance brigade the patronage of the church was returned to the order in 1963.

LANCING *St James the Less* ❀ ✠✠ 📖 (WSSA)150

From the original twelfth century Norman church remain the central part of the west wall and the eastern end of the chancel. Almost all of the rest is fourteenth century, including the central tower and south porch. One of the church's best features is the early twelfth century portal,protected by the later south porch. It contains some excellent stonework, much of it more detailed than was typical of the period. Also of Norman date is the square font decorated with square designs. The early Gothic style of building was reaching its peak when the aisles were built and the octagonal pillars and double-chamfered arches are fine examples. In the fifteenth century the southeast end of the north aisle was blocked off to facilitate the building of a stair turret for the tower, causing an odd-shaped east end to the nave. During the early seventeenth century the church, along with many others at that time, fell into disrepair and the then much taller tower partly collapsed, a Sussex cap was added to the truncated tower to form the tower we see today. In the north wall of the chancel is a fourteenth century tomb recess with a much older grave slab now inserted into it, there is also a low-sided 'sanctus' window to one side. Although in a busy built-up area the church still stands in a quiet corner with a few old houses near by. There are some good eighteenth century gravestones and at least one iron grave marker to the north of the church.

BOTLPHS *St Botolph* ❀❀ ✠✠ 📖 (WSSA)130

The Saxon church of St Peter de Vetere Ponte (St Peter of the old bridge) originally stood at the centre of a thriving village near an ancient bridge, which dated back to Roman times and was the main crossing place of the Adur for over 1000 years. This bridge was so large by medieval times that it had a chapel above the water at its mid point. Due to changes in the river's course the bridge was lost and today only the manor house, a few cottages and the church remain. The rededication to the Saxon bishop St Botolph may have occurred as early as 1080 when the lord of the rape of Bramber set up another St Peter's at Beeding. The original church dates from about 950 and much of the building we see today is from that era. The tall thin walls of the south nave, with one pre-Conquest window and hints of another, and the chancel arch and wall are pure Saxon. The north wall was lost about 1250 when an aisle was added but this was removed within 100 years and the present narrow width of the nave is probably that of the original Saxon building. The now blocked aisle arches are still clearly visible. A little later the apse was removed, the present chancel took its place and the short tower was built. The ancient wooden door bearing the inscription '1630' leads to a simple interior with small fragments of wall paintings, some possibly Saxon. The very ornate Jacobean pulpit with soundboard looks a little out of place but is a fine example of its kind. The royal arms on the west wall are those of Charles II, who certainly passed through Botolphs and Bramber en route to France at the time of his father's death. He may have visited the church and seen fit to bestow his coat of arms on the church after the Restoration. There are two low-sided windows rather than the usual one The three bells in the tower, cast by John Tonne in 1536, are worthy of note and hang in the original wooden frame; both bells and frame have been recently restored. The clean lines of the church with its sparse churchyard combined with an exceptional view make this a perfect setting.

COOMBES ❀❀❀ ✠✠ 📖📖 (WSSA)130

The eleventh century church at Coombes stands in a field sloping back from the River Adur and commands extensive views of the river valley. A few traces of the Saxon building can be found in both the nave, which is mostly eleventh century, and the chancel, which was enlarged in the thirteenth. In the south chancel walls are three fourteenth century windows of note. One contains some original glass with floral designs and another is a very rare round 'low sided window' (now blocked). At the north western end of the nave a perfect example of a deeply splayed twelfth century window survives and there are some fine seventeenth and eighteenth century ledger slabs set in the floor. A few five hundred-year-old coloured floor tiles also survive. The interior of the church is famous for its well-preserved wall paintings uncovered in 1949. These include on the chancel arch soffit a very rare double tranchant design known as a 'Hachette'. This painting includes a struggling figure apparently holding up the arch. Dating from 1135 to 1753 it's the early paintings that are important and rank with other slightly earlier paintings at Clayton and Plumpton. All three churches were probably painted by the monks of Lewes Priory who seemed to have been employed to move from church to church like ecclesiastical interior decorators although their roll was more of the picture storyteller. It is interesting to note that some of the early work was defaced in 1671 when the Ten Commandments were painted on the wall in written form perhaps indicating that it was no longer necessary to portray the message in picture form as more people could read. The roof, a mix of tie beams and trussed rafter, is truly ancient and looks it, as does the font, although opinions differ on the latter's age. Examination of the walls from outside shows several blocked doors and windows but the basic two-cell shape of the Norman church remains unchanged. There is no known dedication for this church but it certainly had one once and there is a hint from an old will that it might have been John the Baptist.

CHURCH DEVELOPMENT THROUGH THE AGES

Few things seem as timeless as a medieval village church. Part of their charm is their stability and the feeling that they have always been there and always will be. The truth is they have survived by constantly changing, sometimes rapidly and sometimes unnoticeably over long periods, but no church remains unchanged. Let us take an amalgam of ancient Sussex churches and look at it as one developing building.

The year is 680 and its isolated position has made Sussex the last pagan stronghold in England. Christianity is not unknown, at least two local kings are either married to Christians or playing safe by following both pagan and Christian beliefs. Dicuil the Irish monk is settled in Bosham, but has failed to make a single convert. He and the few acolytes who came with him have built a small wooden structure which doubles as a church and living accommodation (thought to be on the south side of the present nave at Bosham). One year later St Wilfrid arrives at nearby Selsey with experienced missionaries, builds a larger wooden structure as his headquarters or 'minster' on or close to the site of the present St Wilfrid's chapel and things start to happen.

The missionaries immediately fan out into the countryside to preach at Saxon meeting places and pagan religious sites building small churches on these sites using the authority and financial backing of the Christian kings. Ford church stands on the site of a Saxon meeting place, North Stoke on a pre-Christian religious site and Iford (East Sussex) near the site of a field church. So we have our first building, made of wood, a single room on an east/west axis, with a holy area at the east end. Right from the start this holy area, perhaps just a recess in the east wall was a restricted area where only the priest could go. The new converts were probably told that the new God actually resided in the recess, an idea which would have suited their pagan upbringing.

It's now 880 and little has changed in the style of the church, being made of wood it's been rebuilt several times, each time a little bigger to take the increasing congregation, and some stone work, including a font, has started to appear now that the church is established. The decaying Roman roads spreading out from Chichester have allowed new local born missionaries like St Cuthman, to reach as far as Steyning and start the process over again.

1050 and Saxon England is at its high point and with it Saxon building techniques. Our wooden church is now all stone with tall thin walls; roofs are still thatched or covered with stone slabs. There is still only one door, usually in the west wall and windows are small. The church is the strongest building in the area and is used as a refuge in times of raids. Towers are rare, but some churches have a 'porticus', a cross between a porch and a chapel. In time some of these will grow upwards into the towers we know today. Inside our church a new section has been added to the east, a chancel, totally the province of the priests, even the view from the nave is restricted. The holy of holies is still at the east wall, sometimes in the form of a small curved apse. There are still no seats in the nave and the floor is beaten earth. The dark interior adds to the mysticism so important to early religion.

It is now 1080 and the first Norman king rules England. All the Saxon lords of the manor have gone and new lords from France control the land and the churches.

The fine quality Saxon walls are being replaced with stronger thicker ones, using new methods allowing wider arches; towers are more in evidence. Stone is expensive and hard to work so the old Saxon stones are re-used where possible. The chancel is now screened off completely with a wooden screen; above it is a beam called the rood (Poling), on top of it are statues of the Virgin and the church's patron saint.

Moving on one hundred and fifty years and the apse has gone and a portion of the chancel called the sanctuary has taken over its role. New discoveries in building design have brought in pointed arches, allowing much wider spans. The floor is still not paved and a few stone coffins of important lords and clerics protrude from the nave floor, a stone bench has been added around the nave walls for the sick and old (from this bench comes the term 'to go to the wall') (New Shoreham).

It is now 1300 and in the last one hundred years Sussex has experienced the biggest explosion of church building it will know until the nineteenth century. Money from local lords and the great monastic houses like Chichester has been used to rebuild and refurbish dozens of churches in the new Early English style. Windows are larger but still narrow for glass is expensive or not available. More doors and new aisles have been added to allow for more processions and ceremony. The walls of the nave are brightly painted with descriptive religious scenes and the church is decorated with flowers whenever possible. The nave floor has been paved and the chancel floor is covered with glazed tile.

Eighty years on and the only big changes are the windows. Large windows of the Decorated period, containing intricate stone tracery dividing up the glass panels allow much more light into the church, further reducing the gloominess of the interior.

1460 and the church is smaller now, the north aisle has been demolished after a visitation of the plague reduced the size of congregation. The Perpendicular building style is in fashion and the church has new tall wide windows, with less stonework and more glass, some of it coloured. The separation between the priests and people has declined and limited access to the chancel is allowed at certain times. The first benches have appeared so the congregation can more easily listen to the sermons preached from the new pulpit. These sermons have replaced the short announcements made from the rood loft. The church is rich and established, almost at its peak.

It is 1560 and the unthinkable has happened. The Roman version of Christianity has been swept away almost overnight and the protestant religion has replaced it. The crown has seized virtually all church income and wealth, priests have been thrown out, many churches are empty and derelict, the people are confused. The rood screen and stone altar have been removed by law and the mysticism and ceremony of the old religion has disappeared along with the great monastic houses.

Two hundred years of decay sees our church not just leaking but with large holes in the roof. The Civil War has further damaged the church through vandalism. The new puritan views have caused the removal of all colour and decoration inside the church, even flowers are not allowed. Most rectories had flower gardens prior to the Civil War, the sole purpose of which was to provide decoration for the church. These were sold off or ploughed under during Cromwell's commonwealth mostly never to return. Written references to the flower garden at Kirdford still survive. The standard of priests has declined and only faith keeps the people coming. Permanent stone grave markers have started to appear in the churchyard for the first time which is now, primarily, a burial place rather than a meeting place.

It is now the mid-nineteenth century and the Industrial Revolution has depleted the rural population, but religion has bounced back sparked by the Methodist revival. The churches are packed, modern building methods and government money are leading to the rebuilding and restoration of many churches.

The present day, and much of the old church has been lost over the centuries but a church on the site has survived for over one thousand years by constantly adapting to the local needs and political views at any given time.

ALONG THE RIVER ADUR

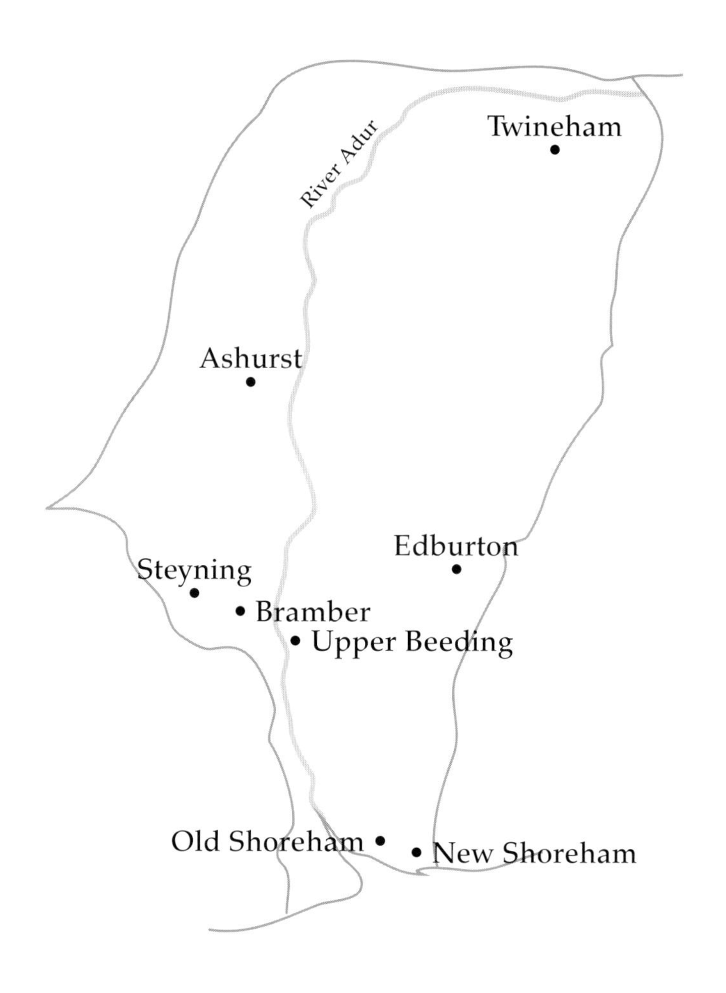

In medieval times the Adur was navigable far inland and Bramber was a major port, as was Shoreham which exported wood as it does today. The castle at Bramber dominated the river and was the centre of power. There have been churches at Steyning and Edburton since Saxon times, with Steyning being the most important church in the area. St Cuthman and King Alfred's father, King Aethelwulf were both buried at Steyning. King Alfred's granddaughter, Edburga, founded the church at Edburton, an area with Royal connections in Saxon England.

STEYNING *St Andrew* ❀ ✠✠✠ 📖📖📖 (WSSA)130

The Saxon church that stood on this spot was built by, and later dedicated to, St Cuthman. The story is that St Cuthman started out from his home in Chidham on a journey intended to spread Christianity deeper into Sussex. He did this pushing his invalid mother on a wheelbarrow-type contraption. At Steyning the rope around his shoulders that helped take the weight broke and St Cuthman took this as a sign from God to stop and build a church at that spot. He built the church, served there all his life and was buried there, possibly in the eighth century. By the twelfth century the area had become very prosperous and the Normans replaced the Saxon church with a massive cruciform building dedicated to St Andrew which stretched further east than it does now and had north and south transepts. A heavy tower stood at the crossing supported by four very tall arches, one of which remains today as the chancel arch. The mid-twelfth century arcades are some of the best Norman work in the country. The arches are decorated with deep cut chevron designs different on each arch, the pillars with scallop and foliage motifs. Above the aisles are sets of clerestory windows still with their rounded Norman heads and separated by palaster strips with a string course below. Combined with the splendid chancel arch the effect is quite impressive. In 1602 the church was in disrepair and the central tower and most of the chancel were removed. Within fifty years the current west tower was added with its chequerboard design. The font is Norman and was reinstalled after being found broken in the churchyard (the result of Civil War vandalism). A prized possession of the church is the sixteenth century reredos of forty-eight oak panels now mounted on the east wall and is a very fine example of Tudor workmanship. In the porch there are two stone coffin lids both believed to be Saxon. One may well have come from St Cuthman's shrine, which was a popular pilgrimage destination. The other is likely to have come from the coffin of King Aethelwulf who died at Steyning in 858. In the street outside the church there is a good modern statue of St Cuthman looking thoughtfully at his church.

BRAMBER *St Nicholas*    (WSSA)130

The church at Bramber stands on the side of the hill on top of which are the ruins of Bramber Castle, and during the life of the castle the two were closely linked. Following the Norman Conquest the entire area was given to William De Braose and he built both castle and church at the same time on the old Roman (and later Saxon) defensive mound. The church, finished in 1073, can claim to be one of the very first Norman churches in the country. De Braose brought in a group of Benedictine monks and set them up as a small monastic community in the castle. A large church was needed to accommodate the monks and the rest of the castle population and a cruciform design was chosen. By 1080 the castle was becoming overcrowded and the monks were moved to another church at nearby Beeding. The church we see today is a shadow of its former self. Both side transepts and the eastern end were lost following damage during the Civil War and a century of disuse. At first sight what we appear to have now is a tall church with a tower at its eastern end. This would be an almost unique position for a tower but closer examination reveals that the tower is in fact not a tower at all. Following restoration in the late eighteenth century the top half of the battlemented tower is in fact hollow and the lower part now forms the chancel. Inside the building the huge chancel arch and its two blocked companions to north and south are evidence of the original shape. The nave is the original Norman structure with a few window changes. The Norman pillars are famous for their almost unique early Norman carvings on the capitals. One appears to show a fox preaching to a flock of geese, this seemingly irreverent motif also appears at another lord's personal church at Etchingham, there it is carved in wood. Another shows a Knights Templar banner and perhaps dates from the time when the Templars had a base in the town. Continue up the hill to the north to visit what was a very large and important castle for almost 400 years. At least two kings, John and Edward I are known to have used the church, (Edward several times).

UPPER BEEDING *St Peter* ❀ ✠✠ 📖📖 (WSSA)130

There was certainly a Saxon church in the area and it must have been built before 858 when Aethelwulf, the father of King Alfred, is recorded as having died'in the parish of Beding' (he was temporarily buried in nearby Steyning. The Norman church which replaced the insubstantial Saxon one was completed in 1073, only months after the completion of nearby Bramber. Both these churches were built by the powerful Norman lord William De Braose and in 1080 he moved a group of French monks to Beeding and a priory house was built on the north side and connected to the church by a cloister. The priory was not large (never more than 16 people and only about 10 of those were clerics). The Norman church was quite small, the north wall followed the present one with the south wall running from a point about .5 metres south of the southern pillar of the tower arch. At the eastern end was an apse, which extended about as far as the present pulpit. By 1283 the church was in poor repair and the monks too poor to rebuild, so the Archbishop of Canterbury devised a scheme whereby the villagers were responsible for the nave, bell ropes and belfry and the monks for the chancel. In 1290 eight leading parishioners, threatened with excommunication for not keeping to this agreement and as a result a massive programme of rebuilding was quickly put into action. By 1308 practically the whole church had been rebuilt with only the tower remaining from the Norman building. The only major changes between 1308 and 1800 were the demolition of the three side chapels. The corona hanging in the nave was made as part of a set for the House of Lords and being surplus to requirements found its way into the church and the font was part of the 1308 rebuild. It is not possible to walk right round the church as the house that stands on the priory foundations takes the ground to the north. The lawns of this house cover the burial area of the monks of the priory and in dry weather the outlines of their graves can clearly be seen in the grass. As usual the often-ignored boundary wall is interesting; this one contains many stones from the old priory.

ASHURST *St James* ❀ ✠✠✠ 📖 (WSSA)110

Ashurst church stands well out of the village in quite heavily wooded countryside. The architectural style is interesting. Early Norman work can still be seen in some walls and the north doorway but most of the church was built about 1220. This dates it right at the point where the Transitional style (1170-1220) was becoming fully Early English (1220-1290). The arches are more pointed but still retain the foliage decoration of the Transitional style while the windows have by this time developed into the true lancets typical of the Early English period. The chancel is the same width as the original short nave with an aisle and arcade added to the nave in the south. Next came the tower, which is short and stocky with an addition to the nave abutting against it to the northwest. The end result is a picturesque group of joined together buildings, all built at roughly the same time, all a little offset from each other and pleasing to the eye both when viewed from inside and outside. Adding to the impression of a group of loosely connected buildings are the roofs, all of which seem to be made of different materials from shingles on the tower's well-proportioned broach spire to a massive single spread of Horsham slabs across the main body of the church. This church roof must be of great weight and is supported by a huge beam stretching across the full width of the nave. On show in the church is a vamphorn. Dated 1770 this is one of only eight remaining in the country, these were used as an accompaniment or to set the key for the hymns. Looking at the simplicity of the instrument the former seems a little unlikely. The oldest part of the churchyard is as usual to the south where there are six very old stones with the skull and crossbones decoration popular in the 1700s. The churchyard has been greatly extended to the north during Victorian times.

OLD SHOREHAM *St Nicolas* ❀❀ ✠✠✠ 📖📖 (WSSA)151

Shoreham was an important local port in Saxon times and its church was impressive by the standards of the time. The original church was built prior to 900AD, was over 50 feet long and had a large tower, which was a rarity in Saxon churches and shows the stature of the town at that time. Some of this very early Saxon work survives in the typically tall nave. The size and position of the early west tower can be seen from its remaining offset walls inside the nave. The original (blocked) Saxon door can still be seen in the old tower wall. The Norman work which forms much of the cruciform church we see today commenced about 1140, a little later than at nearby New Shoreham yet the Transitional style used here would seem to be a little earlier than that used at St Mary's. Inside the church the crossing supporting the Norman tower dominates, and is as good as any in England. Each side of each arch has a different design, as if the mason was producing a catalogue of available patterns. Several heads form the stops, two thought to be King Stephen and his Queen, another possibly the mason himself. There is also a cat's head and elf figure. All the heads and figures seem to have sad or angry expressions. In 1300 the old apsel chancel and its transept bays were removed, as they were at St Mary's, and the present chancel was built in the Early English style. The very rare chancel screen is of this date, as is the coloured tie beam under the Victorian ceiling. An older decorated Norman tie beam supports the roof post in the nave. The main door is the original Norman one in its original position in the south transept but take note of it from the inside where a fine wooden inner porch takes the form of a memorial. In the chancel is a brass memorial to a victim of the Titanic disaster in 1915. The churchyard retains at least part of its pre-Norman round shape and contains some interesting inhabitants including a Russian princess described as an actress who died in 1921. Viewed together the two Shoreham churches offer a unique chance to understand the architectural changes that took place during the Norman era.

NEW SHOREHAM *St Mary De Haura* ❀❀ ✠✠✠ 📖 (WSSA)151

This large and impressive church was started in 1100 when the port of Shoreham was moved here. Although much larger the original plan is the same as the building at Old Shoreham, a cruciform shape with long nave leading to a chancel with rounded apse, and two apsel-shaped chapels facing east in each transept. Originally the nave extended some 40 metres west of the present west door, and the remains of this nave can be seen in the churchyard. The present west door has weathered badly as it was made from softer stone, originally part of the interior. From the 1100-1130 period remain the lower tower, both transepts and the one remaining transept bay. Around the beginning of the thirteenth century the chancel was completely rebuilt on a grand scale and the tower heightened to form a huge church probably intended as a monastic house, what was at the time a massive chancel is evidence of this. The fall from grace of the De Braose family is probably the reason for this church not becoming at least a priory. The length of the church was reduced by almost half when the nave collapsed in the 1700s. Various reasons have been suggested but poor upkeep followed by hurricane force storms known to have hit the town at the time, are the most likely. Although, as mentioned above, a large part has been lost little has been added since 1225 and the impressive flying buttresses are original early examples of this stress-bearing building technique. The building, rather than being in the Transitional style in fashion at the time, is made up of the two very different styles, Norman and Gothic, that came together to form the Transitional style. The tower is half old style, half new and what is now the nave has a north aisle in the Norman style and the south in the Transitional although experts are convinced they were built at the same time. The large round 'wheel' window at the eastern end is only visible from the outside as it looks into the 'attic' between the roof and the ceiling. There is a rare rood piscina high on the wall of the old nave bay, which served an altar in the old rood loft. This church must rate as one of the most impressive parish churches in Sussex.

EDBURTON *St Andrew* ❀❀❀ ✠✠ 📖📖 (WSSA)131

Edburton, a Saxon name, translates as Edburga's town. Edburga (born 900AD) was the granddaughter of King Alfred the Great and is thought to have been instrumental in the building of the first church on the site. A few stones from the Saxon church are incorporated into the walls and there is a very rare tenth century ground piscina (connected to a chain). The present nave was built in 1180 and the chancel and porch added by 1300, all in the Early English style. In 1320 a chantry(now a chapel) was built on the north side and dedicated to St Katherine of Alexandra. The tower came last perhaps as late as 1400 but since then the only exterior additions have been the Victorian windows. The porch is one of the church's treasures, one of the largest and oldest in Sussex it still retains its Horsham slab roof. It's easy to imagine this porch as the busy town meeting place it must have been in medieval times. Council meetings, weddings, business deals, even the school would have been held here. Scratches where arrows were sharpened can be seen in the porch, a reminder that compulsory archery practice was often held in churchyards. Close to the porch are three 'scratch dials'; these simple sundials were used to time the mass and were usually the only form of timekeeping in the village. The church was described as 'exceedingly ruinous' by 1610 and by 1880 a new roof was built as part of a not-too-drastic restoration. The great storm of 1987 again badly damaged the roof and the slab roof was replaced with tiles. The first impression inside the church is how long it is, much longer than most village churches. Just inside the door is the greatest treasure of all, the huge lead font, one of only three in the county and 29 in the land. It dates from 1180, the same date as the nave, and is large enough for total immersion.There is an interesting memorial to the Rev George Keith(d1716) one of the first missionary preachers to go to the American colonies. There are some very old stones in the churchyard plus one rare upright wooden grave marker (now inside the church) uncovered by the author and salvaged for the church during research there.

TWINEHAM *St Peter* ❀❀ ✠✠ 📖📖 (WSSA)92

Twineham means 'between town' and the village and church sit between two arms of the river Adur which was navigable well beyond this point in the past and the village was a busy one as late as the sixteenth century. The present church, which stands on the site of a much older building, was built about 1516, a time of very little church building and is one of the earliest brick-built churches and one of the last pre-Reformation churches to be built. The church stands in a copse of huge oak trees and its churchyard is of great interest. Just inside the main gate is an area marked by four boundary stones, this area was rented in 1694 by the Society of Friends as a burial ground for Quakers and about 60 burials took place here, the last in 1732. The Society of Friends still visit the church every three years to pay their peppercorn rent (the church then pays the Quakers for the use of the hay cut from the area, so all is even). The area is now left virtually undisturbed as a conservation area for wild flowers and animals. Near to the church is a very rare wooden grave board, still in its original state and still readable; to the south is a propeller cross to the memory of a WWI pilot shot down in 1917. Inside the church there is a feeling of a big church scaled down. There is an interesting brass for a pilot killed in 1918, and almost next to it a small stained glass window for another WWI pilot killed 1917 and buried at Ypres. The flattened arches are worth looking at and are typical of this rare late Perpendicular style. The pulpit is Jacobean as is the altar rail and the very fine squire's pew with exceptional carvings is Elizabethan. The pew in front of the pulpit still carries the names of the original households to which it was allotted. The font is thirteenth century and along with the fragments of glass in the SE nave window may well have come from the earlier church. The bell ringers' gallery is particularly nice, giving a clear view into the church for the ringers. Although the west door has been restored the ironwork is almost certainly from the original sixteenth century door and opposite this at the eastern end the reredos contains some thirteenth century carved panels.

NORTHERN VILLAGES

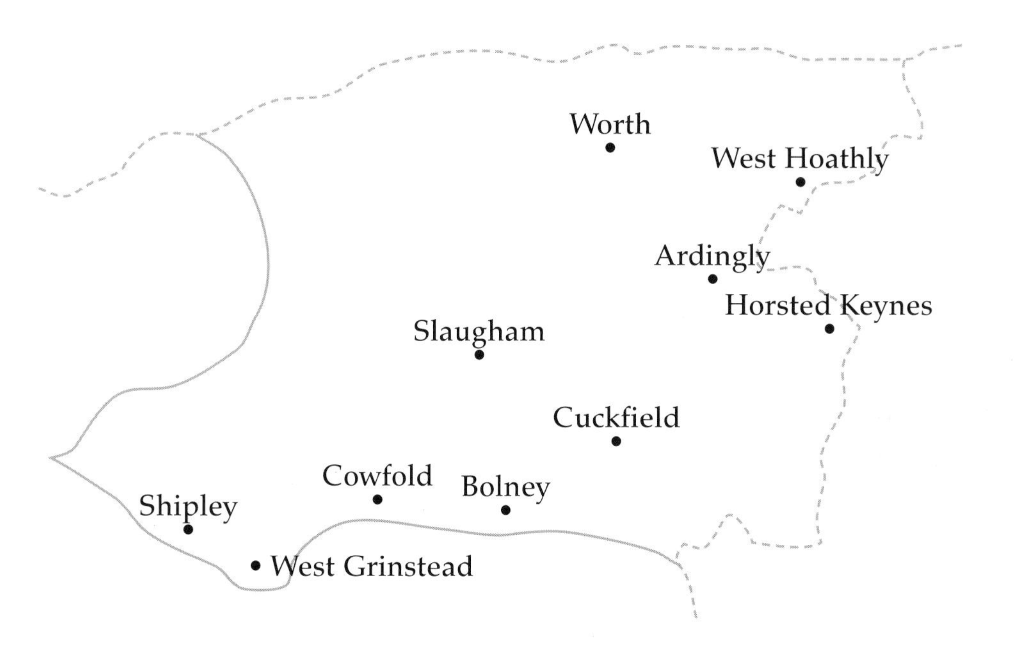

The fine Saxon church at Worth takes pride of place in this area, but Shipley, built by the Knights Templar, and massive Cuckfield with its unique ceiling are not to be missed. Cowfold has one of the best brasses in the land and West Grinstead is steeped in history. Horsted Keynes is built on a pre-Christian site, and at Bolney there is the best example of a lych gate in the county complete with coffin resting stone.

SHIPLEY *St Mary* ❀❀ ✠✠✠ 📖📖 (WSSA)67

Built by the Knights Templar in the late eleventh century this is one of the oldest Norman churches in the county. Although clearly Norman there is a strong Saxon influence in the design. The chancel's tall walls and steep sloping roof would not have looked out of place in a church a hundred years older. The nave and chancel are separated by a massive tower with walls almost three metres thick in places. The medieval spire was removed in 1830, when it became unsafe. The tower arches are beautifully carved with a variety of typical Norman designs, some ending in corbels shaped like grotesque heads. The south walls of the three sections, nave, tower and chancel, each contain one original double-splayed window, rare in a church of this date and once again hinting at Saxon design. The main entrance is now once again the west door, as it was in ancient times, and the doorway is of particularly fine work. Note the beam recesses inside the doorway that once held a large beam that could be slid into place if the church was needed as a place of refuge. High up in one nave wall a small doorway can still be seen. These occur at several large churches in the county and led to rooms above the nave that housed priests who served smaller churches in the area. The chancel, which has a very pronounced twist to the north, contains a large alabaster tomb with life-size effigies of Sir Thomas Caryll (d 1616) and his wife. Also in the chancel is a copy of a thirteenth century reliquary. The fourteenth century south porch protects what must have been the main door in the Middle Ages and contains a medieval bollard which must have been used to secure ships at the nearby river dock that served the village. The north porch of a similar date as the south was removed in the nineteenth century and is now a shed in the churchyard. The large churchyard has its own permanent small flock of sheep, much as it would have done nine hundred years ago. These keep the grass down between the gravestones. John Ireland the composer is buried here, his grave is marked by two prehistoric sarsen stones.

WEST GRINSTEAD *St George* ❀ ✠✠ 📖📖 (WSSA)89

A Saxon timber church is thought to have existed at West Grinstead,where the present lady chapel now stands, but the oldest part of the present building to be seen today is the eleventh century west end of the north wall. During the reign of King John the tower and south aisle were added in the Early English architectural style (1189-1307). This looks to have taken some time to complete and a late change of plan is evident in the widening of the aisle.This work was finally finished in 1272 and the font was probably installed at that time. A little later the chancel was built by the unusual method of removing the east wall and butting on the chancel flush with nave with no dividing wall or arch. The south aisle was extended to form a mortuary chapel (now the Lady Chapel). The excellent examples of table tombs in the chapel now are fifteenth century. There are some very good brasses to be found on these tombs, the best is for Sir Hugh Halsham, a knight who fought with Henry IV at Agincourt. Also from the fifteenth century is the wooden north porch generally regarded as the best in the county, it was built in 1440 at the same time as the fine three-light north window. From the sixteenth century comes the wall painting of St Christopher on the north wall, this painting is usually found in churches that catered to pilgrims so we can assume St George's was on a pilgrim route at that time. The memorial in the south aisle to a member of the Caryll family (Richard, d1701) is of some historical interest. At a time when the Roman Catholic faith was outlawed in England the Caryll's continued to follow the old faith while paying lip service to the new protestant religion. They were for many years instrumental in secretly bringing Catholic priests into the country so that the mass could still be celebrated by those still true to the catholic faith. There is strong evidence that up to twelve Roman Catholic priests were secretly buried in the tower chamber at St George's during this period of religious intolerance. There is a long list of rectors of St George's including the Rev Coventree who was mugged and left for dead in the churchyard over 500 years ago.

COWFOLD *St Peter*   (WSSA)69

This beautifully situated brown sandstone church sits at the centre of the village but off the main road. The oldest surviving parts are the north wall and most of the thirteenth century chancel, which retains some of its original lancet windows. One contains a fourteenth century stained glass representation of the Crucifixion. Several other lancets have been blocked up entirely. Money was left in 1530 for the building of the south chapel which has an unusually complex arch facing the chancel. The arcade is similar but not of such fine work. The chancel arch is a Victorian replacement. The font was bought by the church in 1481, but was made somewhat earlier. The squat tower of pleasing proportions was added in the late fifteenth century, the battlements are perhaps a later addition. By far the church's greatest treasure is the very ornate life-size brass of Thomas Nelond, (d1433) 26th Prior of Lewes. The brass is surrounded by a canopy and inscription band and is almost undamaged. This memorial is one of the best in the country and far too grand to have been made for this church and must have been brought here from Lewes Priory after the Dissolution of the Monasteries in the sixteenth century. Village footpaths divide the tree-lined churchyard, which is very pleasant. It contains a great variation of stones, some very old. Perhaps the churchyard's most interesting feature is the wooden picket fence under trees. Each section still carries the name of the person or farm that was responsible for its upkeep.

SLAUGHAM *St Mary* ❀❀ ⌖ 📖📖📖 (WSSA)48

St Mary's stands in what would in medieval times have been the middle of the almost impenetrable forest that virtually cut Sussex off from the rest of England. Churches were fewer and this church served four villages and still does. From the early Norman church only the north wall and font survive. The font stands on a modern plinth and has a fish decoration on its east face,unique in Sussex. In 1300 the present chancel and lower tower were added. The pillars and arches survive from an early aisle but the large aisle we see today arrived in 1827, adding 200 seats to the church. Also in the chancel are two of the church's four excellent memorials to the Covert family. Both are in the north wall, the first is to Richard (d 1547) and is in the form of an Easter sepulchre, it contains brasses of Richard's three wives in prayer. Next to it is a wall tomb to Jane his granddaughter (d 1586) with a brass of her also in prayer. To the right of the chancel in what was the Covert chapel (built 1613), but is now part of the south aisle, are the other two Covert memorials. The first is a floor brass now mounted in the wall, to John Covert (d 1503). The inscription mentions his will and states that having no son his daughters were to receive large sums only if they married men chosen by his widow. They were to receive less if they married men of their own choice but only if they were in the view of their mother cunning enough to be worth 100 marks. The fourth and most impressive memorial is to another Richard Covert (d 1586). A huge wall tomb carved in heavy relief with seventeen beautifully carved figures depicting Richard, his wife and their fifteen children. The churchyard is extensive and contains many varied and interesting grave markers. To the east are two very rare large wooden grave boards, south east of them are two iron markers that look very like wrought iron gates. The earliest stone is near the Covert chapel and dated 1615; the earliest dated outdoor stone I've ever seen. The large yew tree is over 600 years old and has looked down on almost all the changes made to the church including the extension to the chapel being built now, unusually but quite rightly, in the style of the old church.

CUCKFIELD *Holy Trinity* ❀❀ ⌖ 📖 (WSSA)71

The first mention of a church here is in a Grant document of 1200 when the church of the Holy Trinity Cuckfield was given to the Priory of Lewes. Fifty years later Bishop Richard (later to become St Richard) installed the first full-time vicar and authorised the rebuilding of the small chapel into the first church. Only the foundations of that church remain, the earliest visible parts of the building are the nave end of the south aisle, the lower part of the tower and perhaps part of the south wall. A major re-build occurred in the fourteenth century when the tower was raised and the spire added, the south aisle was extended into the chancel and a north aisle was added. In the same period the chancel was re-built and the two chapels added, the square-headed windows are also of this date. The excellent clerestory windows were covered up in the fifteenth century when the wagon roof was built and not uncovered until 1925. This wagon roof has lent itself well to the unique paintwork done on it and the chancel roof by C.E.Kempe in 1885-86. This work of art is, together with the decorated beams and corbels, clearly the main feature of the church. At least five of the stained glass windows are also by Kempe. While looking at the roof note the small blocked doorway high in the nave, this led to a room above the nave usually used to house priests who served smaller churches in the area. The church fell foul of Cromwell's troops during the Civil War who were responsible for breaking both of the water stoups and causing the large crack in the thirteenth century font. This is said to have been done by the kick of one of the cavalry horses stabled in the church. There are more than a dozen memorials to members of the Burrell family, the earliest for Gerard, vicar of Cuckfield 1483-1509, through Tim the notable diarist, to Percy killed in battle in 1807. There are two brasses for Henry Bowyer (d1588), (one is now covered by carpet). There is an unusual wall plaque to Guy Carleton (d1628), which appears to be made of polished slate. The churchyard contains stones of all ages and types including one nineteenth century wooden grave board restored to perfect condition. There is also an enormous tree, the tallest I've ever seen in a churchyard.

WORTH *St Nicholas* ❀❀ ✠✠✠ 📖📖 (WSSA)11

This church is considered one of the most important Saxon churches still standing in England. Why such a large and impressive church was built in a small clearing of what was at the time one of the densest forests in the land has always been a mystery. With the exception of the nineteenth century tower and the chancel (rebuilt in 1871 using Saxon material) 95% of the stonework at Worth is thought to be Saxon. The building is cruciform in shape,although in common with other churches of the same period the transepts do not quite line up to form a crossing and are in fact two separate chapels. The large size of the apse-shaped chancel makes it almost unique and the chancel arch must have been at the very limit of Saxon arch building dimensions at over 4 metres across. There are signs of rope wear at the top of the arch indicating the existence of a sanctus bell in ages past. The original north and south doorways survive although one is blocked and the other lowered in height. The high Saxon arches of these doorways are still visible and it is thought that they were built so high to allow mounted men to ride in at one, pray without dismounting and leave by the opposite door without turning the horse. Three perfect examples of twin-arched Saxon windows separated by stone baluster shafts survive in the nave and the outside of the church is surrounded by a typical Saxon horizontal string course and vertical palaster strips. Old prints show that the present tower replaced a better-looking short wooden tower that protruded from the north transept supported on timber supports. Following a major roof fire in 1986 the roof was replaced with a lighter framework to reduce the strain on the ancient walls and the only old roof is the one in the south chapel built 1570. The font has been the subject of some debate over the years, originally thought to be twelfth century and standing on top of another older font; recent work has revealed that both top and bottom are thirteenth century and the base is in fact a purpose-built font base. Outside is the final resting place of Robert Whitehead the man who invented the submarine torpedo; somewhat ironic at a church dedicated to the patron saint of seafarers.

ARDINGLY *St Peter* ❀❀ ✠✠ 📖📖 (WSSA)51

Although on the main village high street the church stands some distance from the town. The chunky sixteenth century upper part of the tower gives the whole building a solid look with the heavy slab roof adding to the impression. Viewed from the eastern end it is possible to see how the roof slabs were shaped to fit flat at their base and not laid on at an angle. Some fragments of stonework from the old Norman church are on display in the church but none are still in situ. The nave, chancel and south aisle are all fourteenth century as is the lower part of the tower (the north aisle is a Victorian addition). The rood loft is long gone but the doorway which led to its staircase survives in the north wall. Some interesting old woodwork survives, namely the fifteenth century porch and chancel screen as well as an unusual staircase in the tower cut directly from large baulks of wood. Like nearby Horsted Keynes the church contains many old and interesting memorials both inside and outside the building. In a county not renowned for its church brasses some of the best preserved are to be found here. On the chancel floor are two for the Culpeper family dated 1504 and 1510 but perhaps the best is a canopied brass on top of a large chest tomb which shows Richard Wakehurst (died 1454) and his wife. Both the Wakehurst and Culpeper families were lords of the manor and lived at nearby Wakehurst Place. The oldest memorial is the much damaged effigy of a priest dated 1330. Two of the chancel windows contain some medieval stained glass in the form of shields. Outside the pleasant and leafy churchyard around the church is almost entirely made up of very old stones. A newer extension across the road probably saved these from being removed and replaced with newer burials. A close look round the churchyard reveals almost every stage of development, from the grave board to the modern headstone, only the wooden version is missing. Early gravestone carvings can seem gruesome to modern eyes, skulls, bones and skeletons carrying picks and shovels are often found but one of the most unusual I've ever seen can be found on the northeast side on a stone under a large tree. It clearly shows a skeleton stabbing a reclining woman with a lance while angels look on.

WEST HOATHLY *St Margaret of Antioch* ❀❀ ⌖⌖ 📖 (WSSA)31

This is a perfect example of a church steadily expanding over the centuries to fulfil its local requirements. First laid out in 1090 as a single cell building, possibly with an apse, it extended as far as the small wall projection near the pulpit in length and as far as the present aisle pillars in width. Within 100 years the south a wall was knocked through and a typical Norman arcade installed to give access to a narrow aisle. Another century passes before the chancel is pushed east and a chapel added south of it. A more modern style of arch is inserted to give access from the chancel to the chapel. Soon afterwards the chancel is extended again, the south aisle is widened and linked with the chapel and we end up with a church which has doubled its size in 250 years.

The main door proudly displays its age, with the date 1626 marked out in wrought iron nails, and on entering through it the preserved seventeenth century clock mechanism at once catches the eye. There is a truly ancient parish chest, perhaps as much as 800 years old, its lid lost but still doing service as a table base. There are three very fine examples of iron ledger slabs, all seventeenth century, and all for members of one of the great ironmaster families. There is also a modern memorial to Anne Tree who was burnt at the stake in 1556 for her Protestant beliefs. The rood loft doorway survives high in the twelfth century wall. This gave access to the narrow loft above the rood screen, parts of which are on display in the priest's house museum close to the church. In the chancel are a good sedilia and the north window recesses retain a little of the ancient artwork that must have filled the church in the fourteenth century. Most of the nave roof is fifteenth century and is of a crown post type, the roof in the chapel is older but of a simpler style. The tower was also added in the fifteenth century and was the last major addition. It houses six bells, one carries the verse 'Here am I set on high, By the folks of West Hoathly'. The church dedication, which is quite a rare one, was lost for many years until a thirteenth century document brought it to light in 1937.

HORSTED KEYNES *St Giles* ❀ ✠✠ 📖📖📖 (WSSA)52

When Christianity arrived in Sussex just after 680AD it was common practice to build churches very close to or actually on top of pagan religious sites. St Giles may be one of the best examples of this re-use of a religious site. The original church was almost certainly built on an ancient stone circle, the slight remains of which can be seen in the churchyard. The alignment is far from the normal east to west and may follow the lines of the earlier site aligned to face the rising sun at the summer solstice.From the old Saxon church only the re-sited Saxon door in the north aisle and perhaps the base of the tower remain. The earliest work of any substance to be seen today are parts of the nave and the two round arches under the tower which formed the crossing of the cruciform-shaped Norman church. The apse was removed in the thirteenth century and replaced with the present chancel built in the Early English style with its typical lancet windows. The present chancel arch is a good example of the Decorated period (1300-1350) and replaced the narrower Norman arch. Some nave windows and the pointed arch near the organ are also from this period. The plain fifteenth century font stands as solid as ever in the north aisle. The church is particularly rich in interesting memorials, these span over 700 years and the earliest may be the stone coffin lid set against the wall in the chancel. Also in the chancel is a very rare 'heart shrine'. This takes the form of a miniature effigy of a crusader whose position with legs crossed and feet resting on a lion indicate that he fought and probably died on the crusades. His armour dates him at around 1270. Somewhere in the walls there must be a casket containing the crusader's heart. In the nave is a large memorial to Harold Macmillan the famous post-war Prime Minister who is buried in the churchyard with many of his ancestors. One seemingly very odd memorial is for Henry Pigott who is listed as died March 1715 and born December 1715,a full eight months after he died. In fact the dates are correct, at that time the calendar was different and the new year fell on 25th March.

BOLNEY *St Mary Magdalene* ❀ ⊕⊕ 📖📖 (WSSA)70

The large church at Bolney sits on high ground behind the village and is reached by one of the steep narrow pathways often called 'twittens' in Sussex. The nave and chancel are for the most part pure Norman but it is the tower built in the mid-1500s that dominates the church. Although a pleasant church only the royal coat of arms of Queen Anne is worthy of note (rare in English churches nationally but strangely numerous in Sussex). It seems that all of the interesting features of this church can be experienced from the outside, which is a bonus in these days when many churches are kept locked. The tower contains a peel of eight bells and bell ringing is much in evidence, but if the bell ringers are not in action simply wait for the clock to sound the hour for it not only strikes the hours but chimes as well. Two narrow Norman windows in the chancel are best viewed from outside as is the south doorway which is the church's best feature. Narrower than most church openings, this one is the original Norman doorway with a typical Norman reed-band design around the door arch. The door itself is very old, as is the lock box and large slots in each side of the door arch show where a heavy beam was inserted to bar the door in times of trouble. The churchyard is partly overgrown; this is intentional and is part of a nationwide conservation plan. Searching amongst the long grass can reveal some interesting old gravestones. There are some nice large Victorian tombs and good examples of the transition from wooden to stone grave markers. The old wooden grave boards ran the length of the grave, with the names and dates also running the length of the grave rather than across the head of the grave as is now the case. The transitional markers found here are set the same way with a stone ball or block at each end and a stone bar running between the two. At the entrance to the churchyard is a huge modern lych gate made entirely of local materials. The lych gate (*lych* means *dead body*) is where the coffin traditionally rested during a funeral before being accepted into the church and the lych gate at Bolney still incorporates the central stone coffin rest at shoulder height.

THE VICTORIAN ERA AND ITS EFFECT ON MEDIEVAL CHURCHES

Following Henry VIII's break with Rome in the sixteenth century the political power of the church was greatly weakened and with it went its financial security. The great wealth of the monasteries, the valuable treasures held by churches throughout the country, even the revenue from pilgrims and indulgences were all lost overnight. For the next 200 years churches went into decline with little money to pay for their upkeep.

By the start of the eighteenth century the nation's churches were in a poor state. With the coming of the Industrial Revolution there was a migration of people from the countryside to towns. With the ensuing fall in attendance, there was a further fall in income for the village church and many fell into decay. With some exceptions, the landowner used the church to spend his wealth and maintained the village as his labour force. The latter part of the century saw the rise of Wesleyanism and the Methodist Movement, another move away from the established church but the first signs of resurgence in religion.

The Great Reform Act of 1832 enlightened many aspects of life and made people aware of what was going on and happening in both town and country emphasising the need for change. In 1835, The Ecclesiastical and Revenues Commission started the long process of reforming and revitalising the church. The 1836 Municipal Commutation Act stopped the practice of paying clergy in kind and a series of other reforms by the Church Commissioners re-established the sagging Church of England. It was found that only half of the Church of England's 10,000 properties were occupied. The government now started to intervene, the purchase of vast tracts of land for agricultural and urban redevelopment meant that churches were once again in demand. Not since the mid-seventeenth century had the government taken any interest in the affairs of the church. With the vast income now available and with other reforms, it was secular rather than the ecclesiastical backing that led to the building of 2000 new churches and the renovation of many more.

Religion became part of Victorian life, religion was reborn, and people wanted a sense of belief. The wealthy wanted their mark left on the community and what better way to do it than by financing church improvements, repairs or donating land or items to the church. Many of the new churches were in the new rural communities, the country towns of today.

To begin with the word was 'careful restoration' and the first churches to benefit from the rebuilding grants were put back to their former medieval condition, Upper Beeding is a good example. By the 1860s the Victorian era was quite literally getting its steam up and the medieval church buildings were facing their greatest threat since the Reformation.

This was the age of experiment and invention, anything new was good and the old was out. Now the word was 'rip it out and replace it', if not 'tear it down and re-build it'. Odd and often ugly additions started to appear, tacked on to ancient churches rarely in keeping with the original.

For example, look at the nineteenth century broach spire with dormers and 'frill' added to St. Leonard's at South Stoke, and the renovation of St. Mary the Virgin at Fittleworth which had a complete overhaul and rebuild in 1871. The latter contains some interesting paintings by the rector's son of the work as it progressed. St. Margaret's at Warnham was altered twice in the nineteenth century, in 1847/8 and 1885/6 to improve and enlarge it. All Saints at Plaistow is mid-Victorian and built on the site of a previous church. Some of the interior fittings were saved from that previous church. All Saints at Roffey was built on land provided by the Martyn family, who also paid for the construction. Holy Trinity at Lower Beeding was built in 1840, but is a copy of Littlemore near Oxford and is therefore uncharacteristic of Sussex churches at all. Another church that was extensively altered was St. Mary's at Washington. The church was closed for worship in 1866 and services were held in the vicarage drawing room while it was rebuilt, leaving only the tower and north arcade from the original. It re-opened in April 1867. With Milland, the old church was neglected and a new one, St. Lukes, built only for the original to be discovered and saved many years later.

BRIGHTON'S VILLAGES

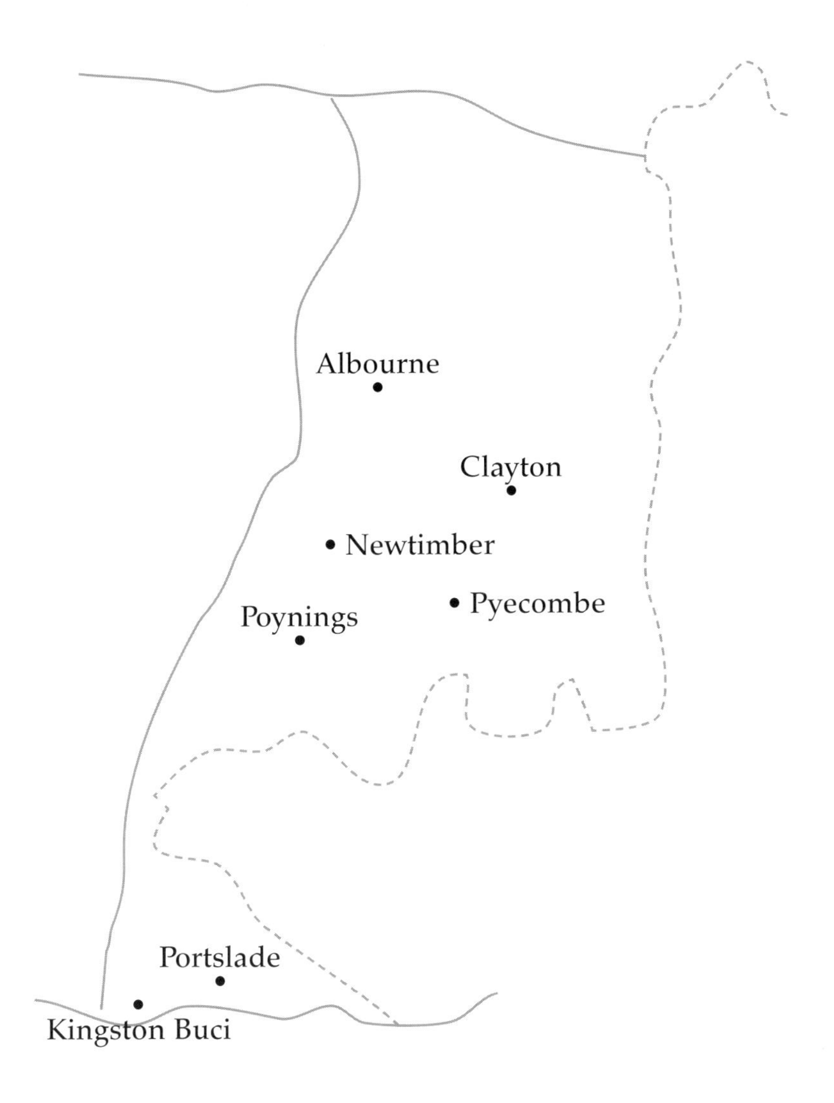

Today, on the east side of the county, the population is concentrated around the city of Brighton; in Medieval times it was a little to the west around the river Adur. The church at Poynings was a manor lord's showpiece and Pyecombe a pilgrims' stopping place. The monastic priory at Lewes held sway over the churches in this area and the paintings at Clayton are the work of Lewes monks and among the best in the country. On the coast Kingston retains the best remains of an anchorite's cell in Sussex.

KINGSTON BUCI *St Julian* ❀ ✝✝ 📖📖

This church is not easy to find as there is no longer a village of Kingston Buci, if there ever was one. The church is tucked away in the modern built-up area of Kingston by Sea, a little-known area between Shoreham and Brighton. The Buci part of the name comes from Ralph De Buci, the Norman lord given the area after 1066. There was certainly a church on the spot when Ralph arrived, foundations were uncovered in the 1960s and much of the present nave is very late Saxon work dating from just before the Norman Conquest. The central but slightly offset tower and the chancel are thirteenth century as was the north aisle (the present one is a nineteenth century rebuild). In the north chancel wall there is a very rare feature indeed, the remains of an anchorite's cell. The cell has long gone but the inmate's viewpoint into the church is perfectly preserved. The door next to it, although said to be part of the cell, worries me a little as true inmates of anchorite cells were walled in for life with no way out. However, if you were paying to be become literally part of the church you could I suppose have a door built into your cell if you wanted, just in case you changed your mind. The inside of the church is very pleasant and contains many interesting items, so much so that the church is often locked but the key is available from the nearby vicarage. Of particular interest is the unique seventeenth century singing desk complete with pitch pipe and the much-restored fourteenth century chancel screen. The Jacobean two-decker pulpit is both impressive and dominating, which is exactly what it was meant to be and has some much older Elizabethan panelling built into it. There are some pleasing-to-the-eye but uncomfortable box pews and two interesting bench ends. The Easter sepulchre in the north wall of the chancel is also a family tomb from the 1600s and has some interesting but defaced carvings of the Resurrection.

The churchyard is small, leafy and a little dark and contains some good stones but nothing of special interest and you do get the feeling that the modern world is crowding in on this lovely ancient church.

PORTSLADE *St Nicolas* ❀ ⌖ 📖📖 (WSSA)152

Portslade is now surrounded by the urban sprawl of nearby Brighton, but was once an important village boasting the largest parish in the area. The first church was built in 1170 and was a small single cell type and from it survive parts of the present nave including the two massive pillars. A narrow aisle was soon added and in 1250 the chancel was built with its slight orientation to the south. The sedilia is from this time and clearly shows the hierarchy of the clergy with its stepped seats. The lower part of the tower was added shortly after but the battlemented top section did not appear until the fourteenth century. Inside the building fragments of what were extensive wall paintings remain. These date from the mid-fifteenth century and cover even older and much simpler work. One of these later paintings is a 'Doom', these frightening representations of hell were much used by early priests to keep their flocks in line. An example of the common church practice of reusing old stone is the floor of the nave which is made up of old gravestones from the churchyard. In the chancel are some good ledger slabs, purpose-made for their present position in the mid eighteenth century. In the south aisle is a brass for Richard Scrase; this brass was brought from the ruins of West Blatchington church. Other memorials show the high mortality rate of children, they show that the lord of the manor lost two wives during childbirth and six children either at birth or in their early years. The Brackenbury chapel was built in 1869 and contains some good heraldic stained glass. These are the coats of arms of the Brackenbury family and the Balliol family (of Oxford University fame) who were closely related. Especially worthy of note in the churchyard are the Buckoll stones with their clear-cut lettering and gruesome decoration, the grave of William Kerr who fought in Wellington's army for 18 years, including the battle of Waterloo, and a large stone for a Norwegian sea captain who died in 1864 not when his ship was lost but when he stepped out of the wrong side of a train and was hit by an express train.

POYNINGS *Holy Trinity* ❀ ✢✢✢ 📖 (WSSA)132

The church was completely re-built in 1369 with money left for the purpose by Michael De Poynings and is a good example of an early Perpendicular-style church. Apart form a little sympathetic restoration in the nineteenth century it remains virtually unchanged these past 650 years. Cruciform in shape with a heavy tower supported on four impressive arches the interior is quite plain and none the worse for it. Most of the windows are original, including the five-light east window, which although clearly Perpendicular in style is simpler than the more ornate ones usually associated with that architectural period. The south transept end window is seventeenth century and came from Chichester cathedral. Some small window sections contain fragments of fifteenth century glass. The unusual octagonal font, with its base shaped to look as if one with the top, is the same age as the church, as is the screen separating the south transept from the crossing. In the south transept are several very old ledger slabs that once held brasses and a stone coffin still with its lid and possibly from an earlier building; this may well be in its original position. This is a rare chance to see what the floor of a medieval church would have looked like, no seats, stone-flagged (if not plain earth) and with a few of these coffins protruding from the floor. Also in the south transept is a wooden beam ornately carved and dated 1623. Other woodwork of interest includes the pulpit, communion rail and family pews all from the seventeenth century and the forty-seven rung ladder in the north transept, parts of which may be as old as the tower. On show is a four-wheeled wooden bier, the best example I've ever seen. Rather than the usual commandment boards hung on the wall, here the verses have been painted onto the plaster itself. The west doorway with its ancient door is worth a look and in the north porch (added just a few years after the church was built) there is some early graffiti on the west windowsill. The church sits on high ground in the middle of the village in the shadow of the famous Sussex beauty spot the 'Devils Dyke'. The leafy graveyard is small but contains some early stones.

NEWTIMBER *St John the Baptist* (WSSA)112

Although much of the nave and chancel are thirteenth century and in the Early English style, and most of the windows are lancets from that period, Victorian re-building and restoration has almost hidden the old church from view. The tower was rebuilt in 1839 and is not a pretty thing with all but two windows blocked up, major re-building in 1875 produced the facade we see today. There are however, many interesting features at Newtimber making it a church worth a visit. To the left as you enter the boundary wall main gate is the tomb of Sydney Charles, Earl Buxton, whose many political offices are listed on a large marble plaque inside the church and include Governor General of South Africa. The most interesting memorial will eventually stand next to Earl Buxton's tomb in the churchyard but at the time of writing has not yet been installed. It will remember the 670 South African tribesmen and their chief who were drowned in the English Channel in 1917 aboard the SS Mendi on their way to fight for England in the First World War. The rest of the churchyard is sparsely populated and a plan and census listing all the known graves can be found on the north wall inside the church. The churchyard contains a large number and variation of trees almost hiding the church from the outside world. Entrance to the church is through the west door of the tower, originally the most common position for the door but now quite rare. Inside the building there are several paintings and drawings of the church before it was rebuilt, showing that it must have looked much like nearby Pyecombe. There are many good wall memorials to the Buxton family, including the previously mentioned marble one for the Earl and a beautiful carved wooden memorial for his son Denis killed in 1917 'leading his men in action'. The pulpit, or at least its panels, are Jacobean although not so ornate as most of that period. The font is nineteenth century. Just behind the font is a block of wood, formerly part of a medieval rood screen, now fixed to the wall to form a shelf for a water container. There are many simple candelabras fixed to the walls and services are still candlelit. The north chapel is interesting in that it was formerly a private family chapel for the manor house at Newtimber Place. One of the bells came from St Swithun's, East Grinstead, who strangely exchanged a good bell for Newtimber's cracked one.

ALBOURNE *St Bartholomew*  (WSSA)112

The church and the nearby Alder stream from which the village takes its name are some distance from the present village and it is quite likely that the ancient village of Albourne was much closer to the church. Only the chancel remains of the Norman church and all the interesting architectural points are to be found there. One blocked Norman window remains as does a thirteenth century piscina. It is also possible that the floor tiles are ancient. Set in the chancel floor is a good ledger slab dated 1711 for a former rector of the parish. The oldest memorial in the church is also set in the floor and is dated 1603. The font is medieval and sits on a massive Sussex marble slab. The chancel is especially interesting as it still gives some clues to the existence of an apse. Most very early churches had this rounded bulge to the chancel which was the holiest place in the church and off limits to all but the priest, but with the lessening of the mystical separation of the clerics and the people these were being removed by late Norman times. A few remain (notably at Worth and Keymer), most have left no trace but here in the east wall the imposts of the former inner arch clearly point to the lost apse. The inside of the church is quite plain and the design of the Victorian nave seems a little odd, as those parishioners sitting on the north side can see nothing at all of the altar or indeed the chancel. Still at least the Victorians did not do their normal thing and demolish the ancient chancel with their 'new must be better than old' beliefs. Probably the church's main treasure is the bell, made in 1285 by Peter the Potter. It is one of the oldest in Sussex and is housed in a small bell turret with a Sussex cap. Outside, the church is pleasing to the eye with its Horsham slab roof and well-kept leafy churchyard. The porch has some interesting carved heads both inside and out, but these are not old and date from the Victorian restoration.

PYECOMBE *The Transfiguration of our Lord* ❀ ✠✠ 📖📖 (WSSA)113

The church and village sit high on a mound only a few metres from the busy main London to Brighton Road. In fact this beautiful country church is no stranger to the passing of heavy traffic. From the prehistoric South Downs track that long pre-dates the church, through the main pilgrims way to Canterbury, to the first staging post on the coach route to London, the site has always been a focal point for travellers. Built in 1170 almost all of the church we see today is original. The thirteenth century tower and porch are the only major structural additions of note. Inside the church is quite plain. There is a rare canopied double piscina (thirteenth century) in the chancel The fine Jacobean three-decker pulpit was rebuilt in 1898 into the present pulpit and rector's stall. The church's two biggest treasures are the ancient encaustic floor tiles in the sanctuary, made in the thirteenth century by monks of Lewes Priory, and the font. The font is one of only three Norman lead fonts in the county, made from a sheet of lead bent into a cylinder and joined at a seam that is invisible even today over eight hundred years later. Traces of whitewash can still be seen on the font from when it was painted to look like stone to avoid it being melted down during the Civil War, to make musket balls. The entrance through the boundary wall is through a fine tapsel gate. Unique to Sussex I have long suspected that the name and design comes from a single family of craftsmen and I have found several gravestones of the Tapsel family in more than one Sussex churchyard. The gate handle is in the form of a shepherd's crook and this is of some significance in Pyecombe. Around 1730 the Pyecombe blacksmith started making ecclesiastical crooks or croziers for bishops. They became the most famous and desirable pastoral staffs and can still be found all over the world. Sadly the smithy closed in the 1970s but the gate latch is a reminder of his art. There is one remaining fifteenth century bell dedicated to St Katherine, could this be a clue to the lost original church dedication? It is said that two other bells were given to the village and church at nearby Clayton in payment of a debt.

CLAYTON *St John the Baptist* ❀ ✠✠✠ 📖📖 (WSSA)113

There is a lot to see at Clayton and it starts at the boundary wall with the lych gate. Built in the early 1920s it acts as the village war memorial and includes one name from the not-too-distant Falklands War. Take note of the church path, it is made of ripple-stone formed from a fossilised riverbed and cut at Horsham. The tall thin nave walls with their long and short work are Saxon and much of the chancel is of the same era. The original dedication of All Saints also hints of Saxon origins. The doorway has been moved from the south wall to the north perhaps to avoid the prevailing wind, but a more recent theory suggests that the original Roman road the church stood next to was on the opposite side of the church from the present road. Churches were more often than not built on the north (or heathen) side of the road and the south door would have opened onto the road. When the road moved so did the door. A blocked arch can be seen in the south wall, which originally led to a thirteenth century chapel the ruins of which can just be seen in the churchyard. The wall paintings inside the church are some of the most important in the country and are true frescoes painted on wet plaster probably by monks from the workshop at Lewes Priory. Like much of the church the important paintings date from the eleventh century, they depict the Day of Judgement and are a forerunner of the more common 'Doom' paintings. There is so much to see here and there is only room to mention a few of the more important features. The medieval door with its hundreds of nail holes from notices; a fine brass under the carpet dated 1508; the eleventh century chancel arch with blocked squints on either side; the window mouldings in the chancel in the form of different, possibly royal heads, and the modern millennium west window, which has received much acclaim, but in my opinion doesn't quite work. The churchyard contains some interesting stones including one military stone from the Falklands War. On a hill to the south two ancient windmills sit close together, they are named Jack and Jill and are believed to be the source of the famous nursery rhyme.

'THE TOP TEN'

hese are the ten churches that score highest using my rating system for - (in order of importance) architectural interest, historical interest and picturesque setting.

1. - Bosham.	It has it all;1000 years of history, incredible architecture,perfect setting.
2. - Poling.	A Saxon church crammed with historical interest.
3. - Boxgrove.	A close third, great history but all of it in one direction.
4. = Sompting.	That famous tower pushes up the score.
4. = Old Shoreham.	The internal stonework takes pride of place here.
4. = Shipley.	A text book for architecture with a Knights Templar history.
7. - Worth.	Unique building, its historical interest and setting let it down.
8. - Climping.	Great history and a great tower, bring a camera in the summer.
9. - Steyning.	Norman grandeur and its own Saint.
10. - Coombes.	Those wall paintings edge it into the top ten.

Close behind come **Edburton, Sullington, Chithurst** and **Yapton**

PATRON SAINTS OF WEST SUSSEX CHURCHES

The Assumption - The belief that when the Virgin Mary died, her body and soul went to heavenly glory.
Cross or Holy Cross - Dedication to Christ on the Cross; the final humiliation and His way of redeeming the sins of Man.
Holy Sepulchre - The cave where Jesus was taken after his crucifixion.
Holy Trinity - The Father, Son and Holy Ghost.
Transfiguration of our Lord - The appearing of Jesus in glory during his earthly life accompanied by Old Testament prophets, as witnessed by Peter, James and John and recorded in the New Testament. (Luke 9, 28-36).
Saint Agatha - 5th century (?) Virgin and martyr, died in Sicily.
All Saints - All the known and unknown Christian martyrs (possibly a dedication of Saxon origin).
Saint Andrew - Apostle who preached in Near East after Christ's death, believed to have been crucified at Patras in Achaia and his body recovered by crusaders in 1204 and returned to Italy. Also thought to have travelled to Scotland and built a church in Fife. Patron saint of Scotland and fishermen.
Saint Anne - Mother of the Virgin Mary, usually depicted teaching the Virgin to read.
Saint Bartholomew - 1st century scholar who preached Christianity in India and Armenia. Said to have been executed at Derbend on the Caspian Sea. Remains eventually returned to Italy. Patron saint of tanners.
Saint Botolph - 7th century bishop of Icanhoe (East Anglia) died 680,probably in Suffolk.
Saint Blaise - 4th century bishop of Sebaste in Armenia tortured with wool combs before being executed.
Saint Clement - 1st century bishop of Rome exiled to the Crimea where he was killed by having an anchor chain wrapped round him and being thrown into the sea. Patron saint of lighthousemen.
Saints Cosmas & Damian - twins who became doctors and Christians, practiced in Africa where they were both martyred. Patron saints of doctors and pharmacists.
Saint George - Replaced Edward the Confessor as patron saint of England after the crusades. Thought to be a soldier who died in Palestine under the persecution of the Christians by Diocletian around 303AD. Patron saint of soldiers, archers, and knights.
Saint Giles - 8th Century hermit who founded a monastery in France, which became a stopping place for pilgrims travelling to the Holy Land. Like St George returning crusaders spread his cult. Patron saint of cripples, lepers, hermits and mothers.
Saint James - one of Christ's apostles executed in 44AD by Herod Agrippa. Preached in Spain. Was adopted by crusaders as defender of the faith. Patron saint of pilgrims.
Saint John the Baptist - John's mother was cousin to the Virgin Mary. He began preaching sometime before Christ, and baptized Christ. Made an enemy of Herod Antipas and his wife who demanded his head for comments he had made. Was arrested and killed without trial.
Saint John the Evangelist - (also known as the Divine) One of the apostles who escaped the persecution of Domitian and lived to old age in Ephesus.
Saint Jude - 1st century apostle who joined with St Simon and preached in Persia ,where both were martyred. Patron saint of lost causes.
Saint Julian - Probably a soldier, who was a devout Christian, and suffered persecution.
Saint Laurence - 3rd century deacon of Rome executed under the persecution of Valerian in 256AD. Recorded his own acts in writing, which his cult follows. Patron saint of deacons, firefighters and cooks.
Saint Leonard - 6th Century hermit, who started life as a nobleman, founded an abbey at Noblac where he died and is buried.
Saint Luke - A Greek physician and disciple of Saint Paul, who may have been a member of

the Christian community at Antioch. Wrote the third Gospel and died at an old age.
Saint Margaret of England - A Cistercian nun, who travelled to the Holy Land, settled in Sauve Benite where she died. Patron saint of dying.
Saint Margaret of Antioch - Probably a fictitious character whose cult was spread by returning crusaders. Said to be the daughter of a pagan priest executed for her Christian beliefs. Patron saint of childbearing.
Saint Martin - born in Hungary, the son of a pagan army officer, joined the army but was discharged for his Christian beliefs, stayed on in France where he worked against paganism. Buried at Tours. Patron saint of beggars and soldiers.
Saint Mary - The Blessed Virgin, mother of Christ. After the death of Christ went to Turkey under the protection of St John where she lived out her life. Patron saint of mothers, nuns, and virgins.
Saint Mary Magdalene - Follower of Christ mentioned throughout the scriptures. Thought to be a sinner. Witnessed the Resurrection. May have been a true apostle but this fact may have been suppressed during the early times of the Christian religion when the role of women was unsure. Patron saint of ladies hairdressers, penitents, and prostitutes.
Saint Matthew - Former tax collector, who joined the apostles, wrote the first gospel and may have preached in Ethiopia. Patron saint of bankers, accountants and taxmen.
Saint Michael - The archangel, messenger and defender of God, his cult usually associated with churches on high ground. Patron saint of radiologists and the sick.
Saint Nicholas - Bishop of Myra in present day Turkey, his remains were brought to Italy in the 11th century, at which time his cult spread throughout Europe. Most famous as Santa Claus, probably due to his custom of giving dowries to poor women on their wedding day and his patronage of children. Patron saint of children, Russia, sailors and pawnbrokers.
Saint Olave - King of Norway (1016-29) and its patron saint.
Saint Pancras - An orphan brought to Rome where he was converted only to be martyred at the age of fourteen. His cult arrived in England in 664 when the Pope sent relics of the saint to King Oswiu, king of Northumbria.
Saint Paul - Nobleman who was converted to Christianity after a vision. Tirelessly tried to spread Christianity until his beheading in Rome at the time of Nero, he was buried outside the walls of Rome.
Saint Peter - Leader of the apostles who preached mostly in Rome. Crucified by Nero possibly at the same time as St Paul as they both share the same saint's day and are often linked together. Patron saint of fishermen.
Saint Stephen - Deacon of the Christian Church, he was a learned man who knew the scriptures. When he accused the people of not supporting Christ, he was stoned to death by the mob.
Saint Sithe - Roman serving girl who gave her master's food to the poor and came to grief because of it. Patron saint of housewives.
Saint Swithun - Bishop of Winchester, where he was educated, and chosen as King Egbert's chaplain. He died in 862 and was buried in the cemetery, but his relics were interred in the cathedral in 971.
Saint Thomas Becket - Archbishop of Canterbury who was killed at his own altar after political differences with the then king of England, Henry II, who was made to do public penance by the Pope.
Saint Wilfrid; Born in c.633, he was educated at Lindisfarne and then went to Canterbury and Rome. On his return to England, had a problem with the existing clergy and was forced into exile and retirement. Converted Sussex to Christianity. Died in 709 at his monastery in Northants
Saint Wulfran - 7th century monk and missionary from France who converted heathen tribes to Christianity with varying degrees of success. Only two churches are dedicated to him in this country.

CHURCH PLAN

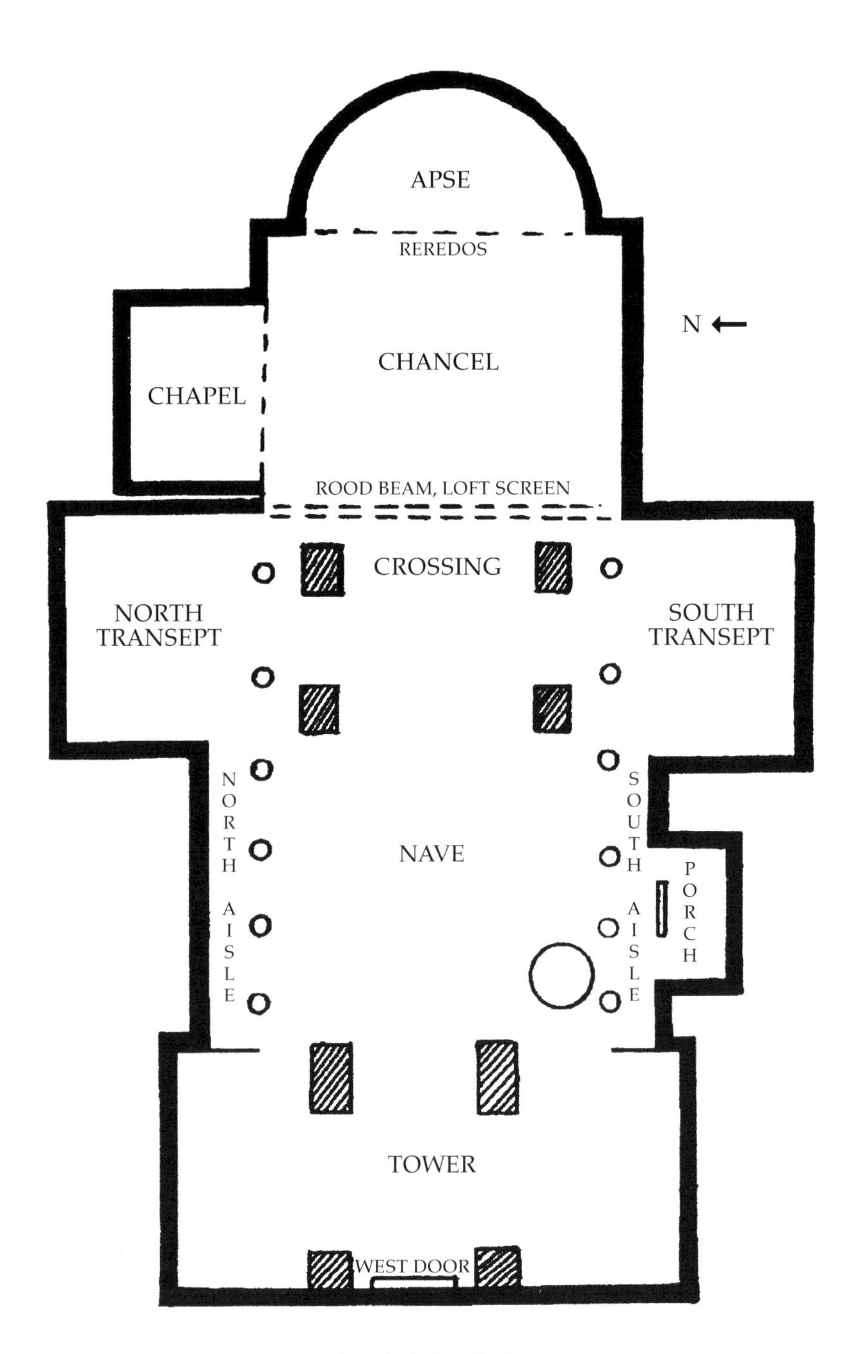

A typical church plan

SUGGESTED TWO AND A HALF HOUR TOURS FOR EACH REGION

WEST DOWNLAND

This tour runs north to south through some of the best scenery in the county.
Start at tiny Chithurst, a timeless building in picturesque setting with the river a stone's throw away. Just along the road is Trotton, full of interesting features including some of the best brasses you will see anywhere. Head south to the three Marden churches, all are worth visits, but if time is short choose North Marden with its rare apse. Continue south to impressive Stoughton and its massive Saxon chancel arch.

WEST OF THE ARUN

Start in the north at Singleton, an important church in Saxon times and retaining so much of its ancient architecture. Travel south-east to Eartham where the history overshadows the architecture. Due south to Yapton, one for the camera, as pretty a picture as you will get. West now to isolated Ford, small but not to be missed. South along the river to Climping, a little of everything here, but the tower dominates.

ARUN VALLEY

Start at Warminghurst, no longer a working church but kept in perfect order and a rare example of its age. West to Wiggonholt or Greatham, both very similar, both candlelit and in remote areas. If there is only time for one, then Greatham. Cross the river Arun to Bury. Very different from the previous two, close to a formerly busy river ferry crossing. Full of architectural changes and a great photo opportunity. Head for Barlavington visiting Coates on the way if there is time. Both are isolated but Barvalington splendidly so, a simple church in a truly rural setting.

ARUNDEL TO WORTHING

This tour runs up the east bank of the Arun across to the Adur and down its west bank. It visits some of the best churches in the county and extra time should be allowed for this premier rated tour.
Start at Saxon Lyminster, then it's just a short drive to Poling, one of the highest rated churches in this book, a winner in every category. Head north with the river to your left; if there is time add Burpham, although this means a detour along a long dead end road, but there are great views of Arundel castle on the way. The main target is North Stoke; this too is down a dead end road, but its well worth the time to see this historic church, now in the hands of the church's conservation trust. Due east from here, (break the journey with a visit to Wiston if there is time) until you reach the river Adur below Steyning. Be sure to take the minor road on the west bank of the river where you will pass both Saxon Botolphs and Coombes with its unique wall paintings. Continue on the same road until it joins the A27, turn west to complete the tour at Sompting with its remarkable tower.

BRIGHTON'S VILLAGES

This tour is surprisingly rural, (at least until the coast is reached) and passes through the famous 'Devil's Dyke' beauty spot.
Start at Pyecombe, stopping place for travellers for centuries. Cross the main London to Brighton road and head towards Poynings. Newtimber is just off the road to the right. Clayton next, to see arguably the best wall paintings in England, then with the famous Jack and Jill windmills of nursery rhyme fame visible on the hills to the south continue to Poynings. Lots of history and interesting features at large cruciform-shaped Poynings. Up over the Devil's Dyke and down to the sea to visit majestic Portslade and Kingston with its anchorite cell.

CHICHESTER'S VILLAGES

The birthplace of Christianity in Sussex this area has much to offer. This is another premier rated tour so please allow extra time.

Start in the east at Barnham, strong on history and architecture. Head towards Chichester to find Westhampnett just to the east of the city. A little of everything here from Roman pipes in the walls to bishops in the churchyard. North again to the interesting church at Aldingbourne, don't forget to try and spot St George on the external north wall. Number three rated Boxgrove next; take your time here, there is much to see. Due west to Westbourne if you are interested in churchyards, this one's the best. Where else to end the tour but Bosham, the number one rated church. Perched on the banks of Chichester harbour, portrayed in the Bayeux tapestry and with truly breathtaking architecture inside it sweeps the board with a perfect score. Take care where you park your car, the tide covers the waterside road twice a day!

NORTHERN VILLAGES

Thanks to the old forest the churches are well spaced out here offering some beautiful scenic drives in between.

Worth is a must, one of the most important Saxon structures still standing in the land. On to Cuckfield with its fantastic ceiling, stopping at Ardingly if there is time. To reach West Grinstead you need to pass Bolney, so take the chance to visit the church and its fine lych gate. The history alone is enough to put West Grinstead on the tour list and it has great architecture as well. End up at Shipley, one of my favourites and very highly rated in this book.

SURREY BORDERS

The ancient forest was thickest here and large areas of woodland still remain, churches like Egdean can take some finding.

Itchingfield with its wooden tower and priest's house start the tour in great style. From here head to Selham, passing Wisborough Green close to the river. Selham is a gem, only its setting stopped it vying for top rated spot in the top ten. Stay south of the old forest to reach Woolbeding, another church strong in all categories. North through the trees to Linchmere, as good a place to end as Itchingfield was to start.

ALONG THE RIVER ADUR

Commerce along the river in medieval times brought great prosperity to the area and the quality of the churches reflects this. Allow extra time for this premier tour.

Start where the river enters the sea. Get a good grasp of architectural styles by comparing New and Old Shoreham. Stay on the east bank of the river to visit the former monastery church at Upper Beeding then cut across to leafy Edburton with its lead font. Backtrack to cross the river near Bramber and climb the hill to see the church and perhaps the ruined castle. End the tour slightly to the north at Steyning, home of St Cuthman and an impressive church by any standards.